Walking through Walls

Proactively challenging barriers in ourselves and society

Catherine Shovlin

Part 1: Introduction…

Cover design by Catherine Shovlin

Part 1: Introduction...

Catherine has enjoyed a career spanning 50 countries and interactions with organisations as diverse as multinational corporations, national government, NGOs, start-ups and the creative sector. She is an astute observer, a lefthanded mathematician and yoga teacher / energy healer, who has raised her 3 children mostly in London, involving them in projects and business meetings as much as travel and creative thinking.

All the individuals who have put walls in my way for me to practice on, contributed to my ability to walk through walls, or who picked me up afterwards.

By the same author and also available on amazon / kindle

Your True Colors

A practical guide to applying color psychology in your life

Live Life in Full Color

A practical guide to balancing your chakras for optimal well-being

Websites:
Windsofdiscovery.com
Changingthelogic.com

Walking through Walls
by Catherine Shovlin

Understanding and challenging barriers within ourselves and in society

Part 1: Introduction…

Table of Contents

Part 1: Introduction…

Part 1: Introduction…

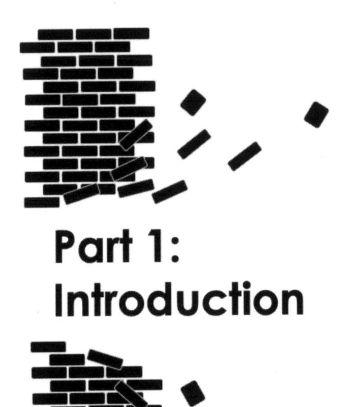

Part 1: Introduction

Why walk through walls?

My motivation

Alfonso dies and goes to heaven where St Peter meets him, welcomes him heartily and gives him a guided tour. The all-you-can-eat buffet, the well-equipped gym, the floating clouds for contemplation and so on.

"Any questions?" he asks Alfonso before leaving him to enjoy eternal bliss.

"Just one. What is behind that big brick wall over there?"

"Oh that's the Catholic section," replies the saintly guide, "They think they're the only ones in here!"

I heard this joke as a child – and practising catholic – and it has remained in a corner of my mind ever since. Unsettling me, giving me pause for thought. And, I now realise, guiding my actions in many areas of life.

A few years ago, during a deep dive process to identify my life purpose, I discovered that my personal mantra, my aim in life, my north star, is **Walking Through Walls**.

Part 1: Introduction…Why walk through walls?

I'm here now to explore this idea with you. Considering the concept of walls. Why we are so keen to create them and some of the hazards they generate. I'm sure you have your own ideas too.

Exploring by storytelling - sharing some of the walls I think we are better off without. Wall stories of my attempts to walk through them. With varying degrees of success. And reflecting, at the end of each story, on the codes to dismantling some of these unnecessary walls so we can live more open, more connected lives – with ourselves, with our friends and family and as a society.

Wall stories?

"Where's the garden chair gone?" asks Liz who is helping me with some much-needed maintenance of my unruly back garden. She pushes her unruly ginger curls out of her eyes with the back of a rough gardening glove.

"Oh, I remember, I lent it to the neighbours for a party"

A minute later I hand it back over the wall to her before jumping back to the home-side myself.

Part 1: Introduction…Why walk through walls?

"You don't even see barriers do you?" she laughs. And I realise she is right. I haven't even considered the wall.

In another conversation in the same garden, Patricio is, to my utter amazement, asking me to be a director of his company creating public artworks.

"But why me?" I can't help asking.

"Because you laugh in the face of challenges" is his unexpected reply.

In one of our first projects together we were creating an artwork of imaginary books that members of the local community would like to read or write. The title of my own imaginary book was immediately obvious to me. "Walking through Walls".

That artwork has adorned the community library ever since, and it has taken me ten years to get to the task… but here we have it, the codes for walking through some of the walls we encounter.

War stories are an established tradition. For millennia they have been shared. To learn lessons, to build reputations, to influence others. Many of us, myself included, have not been to war. But we all have our share of *wall stories*.

Part 1: Introduction...Why walk through walls?

It is my proposal to you that we can benefit from greater awareness of the walls we have around us. Some of which we have built ourselves and some that were handed to us by others. By opening our eyes to these walls we create a choice. Are we happy with them? Do they serve a purpose? Or are they no longer useful and can be cheerfully – or through gritted teeth – kicked down to open up the space and allow new possibilities to flow.

Imagine trying to create a delicious meal if there were walls between each of the ingredients. The flavours barred from combining and enriching each other. The finished product a collection of parts instead of a symphony of all. It would be a terrible shame and so many delightful combinations of flavours would be lost.

It is clear here why walls are not always helpful. But in the rest of our lives we might have long since stopped noticing them and not realise what they are doing to us or to our families, workplaces and communities. Let's open our eyes. Let's open our minds. Let's open our hearts.

Walls promote ignorance, division, *Othering*. They reduce circulation and restrict freedom. They may seem protective but what if all they are doing is "protecting" us

Part 1: Introduction…Why walk through walls?

from a better world? Or making sure we don't realise how much better things are on the other side.

For each of the Wall Stories I will conclude with a summary box of the

- **Cause** of the wall existing
- **Consequences** of the wall
- **Code** to start to walk through the wall
- **Benefits** of dismantling the wall

In celebration of over 30 years since the demolition of the Berlin Wall – and flying in the face of the other walls being threatened across the globe in the name of protecting economies or health – let's explore Walking Through Walls together.

Part 2: Why do Walls Matter?

Good reasons for walls

Some of the earliest walls were for protection. A wall around the huddle of makeshift homes around the fire, to keep out wild animals. A wall around a small town to make it easier, and less labour intensive, to protect its occupants while some of the stronger members were out hunting or exploring. At this stage the wall was largely practical. Not a place to hang art or express your preferred colour scheme. Just a simple way to keep warm and dry and safe.

I'm not suggesting that walls are always bad. Of course they have a role to play. Though they do always evidence a shift towards increasing control or a sense – maybe a false sense – of ownership.

When early men built a wall around a patch of ground and put animals inside it, instead of allowing them to roam free, they were starting a cycle of intervention that would bring us all the way to genetically modified animals living separately in confined spaces to minimise disease and maximise production of market quality meat or dairy. The balance of control shifted from the animal towards human.

And in that shift from growing food to a more formalised agricultural system, it also shifted power towards men, coinciding with the replacement of female deities (representing nature, abundance, fertility and so on) with male ones relating to conquering lands and gaining power.

Mission creep with walls

Walls then began to be used to define territories.

Walled cities, a physical representation of the city state, developed from the 8th century BC– both to define the cities and to protect the accumulated wealth inside. There are examples in all continents of walls starting to be used in this way thousands of years ago. Creating a sense of insiders and outsiders. Those within the city wall – protected but also controlled in some senses – and those without, taking their chances on the outside.

Hadrian's Wall built nearly 2000 years ago in the UK, close to the present-day border between England and Scotland, was a marker for the edge of the Roman Empire. It was not cost effective for the Roman Army to take on the wilder folk north of the wall, and no doubt they were already at the limits of their tolerance for cold weather – socks and sandals will only take you so far!

Negative impacts of modern walls

We see, in modern cities, that as soon as a railway line or highway divides a town, different characteristics begin to emerge on either side. Until the railway line is constructed, coming from "the wrong side of the tracks" would not have been such a stark marker. So putting in a wall starts to create distinctions between one side and the other. Maybe subtly at first but with increasing emphasis until everybody understands the social and economic meaning of one side versus the other.

The "peacelines" used in Northern Ireland – physical markers – are associated with increased levels of mental health problems as identified by Aideen Maguire in her research on the topic. Restricted movement is not natural for any species, including humans and when it is used to define haves and have nots, such as the segregation walls built in cities all over the USA to divide black and white neighbourhoods, it generates a host of repercussions.

The case for challenging walls within and around cities seems pretty clear to me. But I am not restricting this discussion to walls made of bricks and mortar. Through decades of working with large organisations I have

Part 2: Why do Walls Matter?...Negative impacts of modern walls

repeatedly observed the compromises, distortions and loss of efficiency caused by organisational walls. Like the separated ingredients in the earlier cooking example, this degree of separation stifles creativity, integration and joined up thinking. It can create situations where optimising a situation inside one wall creates widescale problems in the rest of the organisation – a consequence that might have been obvious if anybody had tried to look over the wall... or even walk through it.

Closer to home we will observe the walls we create between and within families, generations, gender, health conditions, talents and challenges. This is rich territory for reflection. For a while you may feel that everywhere you look there are walls. Take heart, becoming aware is a valuable first step. You are starting to see invisible walls – until you do that you cannot decide if you want them there or not.

And lastly, we will look inside our own city state. Our own heart and mind. What walls have we built inside ourselves? And how might we be better off if we walked through them? Freer? Happier? Better able to make a positive contribution to the world?

Part 2: Why do Walls Matter?...Negative impacts of modern walls

For clarity, I have organised the Wall Stories under three headings – society, organisations and ourselves. Though as you will see, they are each mirrors of the other and lessons carry across them all.

Part 3: Walls in our World…Negative impacts of modern walls

Part 3: Walls in our World

Context

Let's start with the most visible aspect of this concept – the walls in the world at large. The walls we see between groups of people in society.

Let's start there because it's always easier to see what's wrong with something on the outside. We can be the observer, the witness, the analyst.

In the outside world, the consequences of walls are writ large and the unnecessary human suffering is hard to deny. Armed with that motivation to make change we can later turn inwards and see how we can start with ourselves.

In this section we will consider walls in society in its broadest sense, and then in Part 4 we look at walls in organisations. Lastly in Part 5 we will consider the walls inside our own hearts and minds.

All three are important to be aware of and to challenge. It is hard to change society without addressing ourselves. As Mahatma Gandhi advised, *"Be the change you want to see in the world"*.

The Wall of Distrust

When the council announced they were going to close our local library – in an area of multiple deprivation with very low computer ownership – there was an outcry. A campaign group formed. They raged, they staged protests, they gathered signatures, they organised sit-ins.

All to no avail. The council locked the doors in July and announced that they would rent out the high street premises as a discount store. We, the local community and the campaigners, had to understand that this was a prime location and could generate a useful income for the council. We observed that the same might be said of several schools, clinics and children's playgrounds in the neighbourhood. The logical conclusion would be to abandon all public services and operate the local council as a land bank / property company. But wait, that's not what they're for is it? This profit argument didn't hold water. And nobody was about to give up.

The campaign group step up their actions and offer to run the library themselves as volunteers funded by donations. Four other libraries in the district are being handed over to voluntary groups so there is precedent. Certainly not, retort the council, expressing concerns over the capacity, legitimacy and sustainability of the campaigners. Battle lines are drawn and from where the council sit, it looks a lot like the campaigners are the enemy. The same is true for the campaigners who are taking a dim and increasingly sceptical view of the council.

I get a call from a concerned local councillor. As one of the founder directors of a community charity in the same neighbourhood, he wonders if maybe we might intervene?

This is a controversial option. At a time of widespread cutbacks from a right-wing government, taking on the library feels like an endorsement of austerity measures and acquiescence to the dismantling of the welfare state. Most people in the area are opposed both to the current government and to the austerity program. We cannot be the government's lackey! We have higher principles!

On the other hand, I argue, these principles are something of a middle-class luxury. We live in comfortable spacious houses with more books than we can ever read and multiple devices to access the internet. That isn't the case for a lot of the people using the library. Can we live with the idea of sacrificing their well-being on the altar of our principles? Something doesn't sit right.

We run an anonymous online conversation to step away from the personalities and bottom out some of these arguments. By a process of consensus building, the conclusion is that while we stand firmly against the cuts, we stand even more firmly with the rights of local kids, vulnerable adults and those needing computer access to interface with the government benefits system (social payments for disability, retirees, carers, those out of work etc).

Now to walk through the wall between the campaigners and the local government officials.

The campaigners are clearly the people to run the space, and the council are the ones with the keys to the building. By this stage they neither like nor trust each other.

At first, I am sitting on top of the wall, looking both ways. At concerned, caution-driven government employees on one side of the wall – for whom a decision represents all risk and no upside. And at enraged local citizens on the other, whose only conclusion is that the council are heartless bureaucrats, the enemy of the people. From where I sit, they both have reasons that make sense to them for taking a strong position.

Most of the first meetings are me with one party explaining the motives and intentions of the other, then going back to the other party to do the same. They can't be in the same room as each other until this groundwork is done. To a limited extent they start to consider the remote possibility that those on the other side of the wall might have their reasons for behaving badly. At one point the council suggest a meeting – with biscuits (cookies)! They add, as a curious inducement. Maybe this is how things work in local government? I'll see you a cookie and raise you a muffin!

We convene a community meeting, in the library space, with the campaigners, council and members of the public together. Late afternoon sunlight streams through the glass frontage, highlighting the stained and missing ceiling tiles, worn carpet and shabby furniture. The books stand in puzzled silence missing the excitement of being thumbed through and then returned to the wrong place in the Dewey Decimal system.

The meeting quickly shows all the signs of descending into an ugly wrangling of moot points.

Until we spot a chink in the wall when the council express their regret that they will be one library down for the Summer Reading Challenge (a nationwide program which encourages children to read in the school holidays in return for badges and fun activities). Taking a chance, and with no consultation, I lean forward on my only slightly wobbly orange plastic chair and suggest we drop the campaign for the library (withstanding the kicks in my shins from the campaigners) and instead just help the council out by opening the doors for six weeks for the Summer Reading Challenge and running it for them. Not offering library services. Not re-opening the library. Just using the space so the Reading Challenge can take place and showing good faith and an intention to support the local community on both sides.

In front of the local parents that proves to be an impossible offer for the council to refuse and we are allowed to have the keys to this gleaming emporium for six weeks.

Roll forward almost ten years and the community library and learning space are still going strong. User numbers are up, especially among non-traditional users of libraries eg non-English speakers, people with literacy issues, people with mental, social or physical disabilities and lower income families. The whole place has been redecorated with volunteer labour and donated paint. We fundraised to fix the ceiling and the carpet and crowdfunded to create two artwork spaces in the ceiling for local groups to display the creativity.

The stories of personal transformation of volunteers and users with multiple needs are many and inspiring, and the local council proudly presents the case at national conferences as an example of cooperation with communities. We just smile graciously.

Knocking out that first brick in the wall, creating a six-week trust experiment, allowed mutual confidence to start to grow. Over the years of consistent operation and successful innovation, that trust and mutual confidence has continued and strengthened to something that feels a lot more like a partnership.

Wall of Distrust	
CAUSE: lack of understanding of or belief in other's motives	**COST:** sub-optimal arrangements, squandered resources
Walking through the wall	
CODE: *listen* to each other with an open heart, look for third way. Take a leap of faith.	**BENEFITS**: new possibilities, better solutions, volunteers now in paid work, homeless people signposted to services they weren't aware of, local schoolchildren given a sanctuary in case of bullying, new skills learnt…

The Wall of Fear

The gentle breeze offers scant relief from the baking heat in the dusty square of a small mountain village in Northern Lebanon. A mixture of Lebanese women who have always lived here, and the more recent arrivals from across the border – refugees from the Syrian crisis gather in a makeshift circle of orange crates and plastic chairs. They have all been living in the same village for a couple of years now, but still aren't entirely sure how to treat each other.

I look around the circle. The women are shuffling awkwardly, staring at the ground. There is little sign of the cheery welcome I am used to seeing in the refugee-only circles I have run. The olive trees rustle with curiosity.

There are a lot of historical cultural and social bonds between Syria and Lebanon. There have been centuries of exchange of goods, wives and skills across the border over the centuries. As well as a more recent history of Syria occupying Lebanon (1976-2005). There is also of course tension generated by the presence of two million refugees on top of a local population of only four million with all the pressure that puts on jobs, the water supply and public services.

We start our <u>Hope Circle</u> (see hopecircles.org for more information, or my Udemy course on Trauma Release to find out how to run your own). I have used this technique in several different contexts to encourage listening, trauma release and create connection. It is a simple technology, easily learned by the groups I work with.

It is immediately apparent that there is a strong context of fear. Fear of the past and its memories for the Syrians. Fear of the future too (what will become of us? Will we ever go home?). Fear from the Lebanese (will they take all the jobs? Will they ever go home?). A shared experience of fear of fathers, fear for sons. Fear of being swallowed by grief. Fear of gossip. Fear of hopelessness.

Despite this common ground, the women do not offer each other solace or feel safe confiding their problems. Fear of not being able to handle someone else's problems as well as my own maybe. Fear of being humiliated. Fear of being laughed at. Fear of showing weakness and being vulnerable. An acute case of emotions we have all felt. Despite our physical proximity in the circle there is no closeness.

Breathe. I remind myself first to breathe, both feet flat on the floor, hands on my belly. Breathe into the discomfort. Breathe into my own fears of not finding a way for this circle to become something that can help. Breathe into the space we are sitting in. Breathe love towards each and every woman in the circle.

I encourage the women to do the same. Sidestepping the issues for a moment, just focusing on being. The breath of life that we all share. Allowing it to enter and leave our bodies in a slow rhythm. As our breath synchronises, I feel that subtle shift in the energy of the space that is always a sign of hope for me. Of possibility. It feels like filaments connecting the women, one by one, some faster than others, some wary, the web between them gathering substance with every moment of listening, of seeing the other.

We start the circle. Passing around the talking bowl. Giving each woman space and acknowledging what she shares. No judgment, no come back, no suggestions, no mirrored experiences. Just space to talk. Space to be heard. Space to be accepted exactly as you are. By a combination of rounds of the Hope Circle and sharing some simple trauma release techniques we start to melt the wall of fear that they each have around them.

Part 3: Walls in our World…The Wall of Fear

By the end of the Hope Circle, after laughter and tears, they each speak of the relief they feel from opening their hearts and realising they *can* be there for each other. That they can allow each other in. That they have more in common than they have distinctions. That my pain is your pain. And I can hold your pain for a moment and give you some relief. And vice versa. That we can help each other without diminishing our own ability to cope – indeed nurturing our own resilience in the process. Finding fullness.

The supportive embrace of a shared experience. As the walls between them start to come down they look into the eyes and hearts of the other women – and realise that they are not to be feared. They are to be honoured, comforted, supported, seen. Each to the other. Each for the other. Each with the other.

"I lost all of my family in the war," says one, eyes bright with emotion. "And now for the first time I realise I can make a new family. Right here. You are my family now. And I am yours. I no longer feel so alone."

Wall of Fear	
CAUSE: past trauma, sense of otherness, suspicion, fear	**COST:** loneliness, sadness, hard to heal wounds, trapped emotions unleashed on their children as harsh words and slaps, shrinking
Walking through the wall	
CODE: simply *listen* to each other with open hearts	**BENEFITS:** friendship, support, healing, more ability to cope with hardship

The Wall of Superiority

"What's wrong with these stupid people!" exclaims the senior civil servant in the Dept of Education. "Can't they see what's good for them? We've told them often enough!"

They have brought me in to develop the story, and therefore the marketing materials for a new learning grant designed to address the UK's skills gap compared to its competitors. How it has become a country with world-renowned universities yet missing a strong technically skilled population – a key ingredient in Germany's economic success.

"Can you go and talk to them?" they ask, "Because frankly we find them a bit scary in their council flats with their regional accents. We just don't know anybody like that. They don't even go to France for their summer holidays!" Just as well, I think, wondering how quickly that conversation would descend into the patronising vs the furious.

And so I set off around the country. Meeting up with kids from the chip shop queue, the video store, the bus stop.

Talking to teenage mums in council flats, sitting on the floor of the community centre with newly imported wives from Bangladesh and buying seasonal workers a beer in the pub in return for talking to me. Meeting people on their own ground and talking to them in their own language. Spending time understanding how the world looks from their point of view. Who they trust and who is "out to get them". Their role models and fear models. Their hopes and dreams and frustrations.

What quickly becomes clear is that none of these people get up in the morning thinking "How can I ruin my life today?" Whatever they do, and however foolish it seems to the education providers, they have their reasons. Maybe not well-informed ones, maybe coming from a lack of self-esteem or good information or poor role models, but nonetheless they are making the choices that make most sense to them based on the information that they have.

So long as the Dept of Education hide behind their Wall of Superiority and issue bossy or patronising leaflets to this target audience, this is never going to change. The people they aim to help are being treated like they are wrong, in many ways they already feel wrong, and they feel stuck in this set up where the odds are stacked against "people like me".

The first and most effective rule in these conversation groups is that of "no wrong answers". Want to burn down the school? OK let's talk about that. Boom. It's gone. What next? Do you want to build a new school? A different sort of school? What will it be like?

What about jobs? Who do you know who's doing ok? So you want to be a drug dealer? Let's talk about that. Who else do you know who enjoys their work? The widespread lack of role models is abundantly clear… with the exception of a scattering of single aunts who seem to be the only people they knew who are working as nurses, teachers, or doing something more interesting and satisfying than what they call a dead-end job with no prospect of a brighter future.

Scared of going to see the careers teacher? Embarrassed to be seen to be trying? No idea where to start? Let's talk about that.

Mystified by being in a new country with a new husband, and scared of your live-in mother-in-law? Then let's talk about how you could still do something that works for you.

Part 3: Walls in our World…The Wall of Superiority

Many of the people I meet aren't used to being treated as though they might be right. As though their views are valid and reasonable even when they are self-destructive. It gets their attention to make this the game. Even the quieter ones start to speak up once they realise this is a safe space. The agitated ones settle down. The angry ones relax a bit.

Another key factor to walking through this wall is when they realise that I have no agenda beyond understanding something about them. That I am their advocate not their inspector. That I can inform the people who want to help and see if we can tailor things to be more appropriate and relevant.

The next breakthrough comes when I heave a stack of about 100 leaflets I have gathered from schools, libraries, the Post Office, colleges and job centres onto the table.

"Imagine that lot just dropped through your letterbox," I explain, "Now you get to see what you think."

Their eyes light up when I tell them they can throw the ones they don't like onto the floor.

"Brilliant!" they enthuse. The judged become the judges.

Shockingly, 85% of the leaflets are rejected by EVERY one of the dozens of young people I speak to, no matter what their gender, race or location. This astonishing mismatch of message to audience is clarified when I profile the young people as well as those people providing training options. On all four measures of motivation and attitude they are the exact opposite of each other.

Something very common is going on here. The well-meaning folks putting together the leaflets, are using concepts, language and imagery that would work for them. But that messaging is mostly falling on deaf ears with their target audience who have completely different filters in place.

"Too boring"

"Fake"

"Doesn't tell me what to do"

"Too cheerful"

"Drab. Horrible colours"

"Too council"

"Just catalogue people, not real people"

They are very clear about their reasoning as the leaflets are tossed onto the floor.

Of the remaining 15 or so survivors, many are wounded. Damned with faint praise.

"I suppose that one might be helpful. To someone. Not me though!"

"At least that one's got a website instead of expecting you to phone someone. I'd never do that!"

In the end out of over 100 leaflets, there are only 3 that more than half of the target audience agree are worth considering.

This is very important learning. In a situation where interest in further education are worryingly low and a large number of young people end up not in employment, education or training – or in dead end jobs that will teach them nothing and offer no prospects, it is vitally important that a more impactful conversation take place.

Breaking down this wall depends on smart language and behaviour profiling.

When I assess all of the data from all of the conversations, I see that the young people's typical profile is pretty much the mirror image of that of the civil servants, teachers and careers advisers. And, as you would expect, the literature is almost always a match for those commissioning the leaflets – those peddling education – and, because of this mirror profile, invisible or meaningless to the young people it is intending to influence. It is literally going in one ear and out the other. Bouncing through without any chance to influence the reluctant recipient. A waste of time and resources as well as actively damaging the connection between the educators and the young people since it acts as evidence that "they have no idea".

Getting the young people involved to co-create the literature is dramatically more successful. They choose strong colours and bold graphics. Headlines which speak to their worst fears "Don't get stuck in a rut", "Don't get left behind" – grab their attention. The least number of words possible and all straightforward, honest, direct they insist. No "youth speak" or complex ambiguities. No false optimism or wild promises that "the world is your oyster" when they feel trapped and hopeless. Being told there are thousands of options is just overwhelming.

What they do want are a maximum of four clear next steps to follow. Photos of cool, attractive young people but not *too* cool or attractive. People they can relate to.

People they might know. The job of the leaflet and the posters is simply to get them to the next step, not to map out their entire life. Grounded, trustworthy and "about me, for me".

Despite their reservations the Department of Education decide to risk this approach in a pilot area. All credit to them since the mirror is working the other way now and they feel deeply uncomfortable with the materials. They are especially hesitant about the one targeted at the Bangladeshi wives until I suggest they walk it round their Asian staff. They call me back an hour later. "They love it!" they report with astonishment. "They said they felt recognised and understood for the first time ever."

Once the new campaign is up and running, the enquiry rate for further education and training increases ten-fold. That's the power of telling people things they can hear in a way that respects their point of view and makes it clear how to proceed.

Wall of Superiority

CAUSE: lack of awareness of other points of view, or seeing them as not valid, misguided or wrong	**COST:** outcasts, self-fulfilling failure, poor solutions, high social cost of under-actualised individuals, higher rates of depression, addiction and dependency on the state

Walking through the wall

CODE: *listen* to the party being seen as inferior, meet them where they are, travel to their world and see the view from there	**BENEFITS:** talk about solutions in ways that work for recipients not providers, increased motivation to learn skills, creating scope for better life outcomes / well-being

The Wall of Death

I travel a lot and have spent time in different cultures in Asia, Africa and the Middle East where death is still seen as an integral part of life. Meanwhile in the West we have tended to push it further and further out of sight. Deaths in hospital have become the norm rather than the exception. Many are not sure if they are even allowed to spend the last days and weeks having their loved ones at home. And once death occurs, the body is often whisked away as soon as possible to be "dealt with" by the professionals.

In general, our degree of sophistication and civilisation has created a world where discussion of death is seen as morbid and in rather poor taste. In a world of anti-ageing creams, face lifts and hair dye, getting older is often seen as a bit of a personal failure. Letting the side down, letting yourself go. Growing old gracefully has come to be seen as a cop out and forever young and forever alive seems to be the unspoken expectation – even though we all know only too well that cheating death has an abysmally low success rate. It gets us all in the end.

The medical profession too, with increasing access to interventions and a duty to do everything possible to prolong life, are caught in a bind. A friend of mine is a senior hospital doctor specialising in pulmonary disease so sees a lot of elderly patients. She described to me how it often felt cruel to keep people alive long after they were ready to slip away. And that even when the patient is ready to go the family are unable to release their attachment and beg her to do anything she can to keep their loved one alive.

There is a way round this, to have an Advanced Plan (called a Living Will in some countries) where you can specify, well before the likely event, exactly what measures under what conditions you want to have applied to you. For example while you are a mother of young children and have been in a car accident, you may well want whatever they can do. But if you are in your 90s, feel that you have completed your life and don't like the idea of being bed ridden and in pain for more time, your perspective could well be different. I strongly recommend completing such a plan, though I recognise that for many people it feels like 'tempting fate', making death more likely by even just mentioning the word. It is worth noting however that the highest suicide rates in the

USA are among males over 75. Taking matters into their own hands?

In 2020, the COVID-19 virus challenged this western attitude to our own mortality. Death stepped out of the shadows and became, not just something that happens to other people, but something that might happen to ourselves. This was a considerable shock to many in the West, unused as we are to the day to day expectation of death found in communities with high infant mortality, minimal health and safety procedures and a surplus of tropical diseases and natural disasters.

For me the most compelling aspect of my two-year training to become an End of Life Doula – someone who walks alongside the dying on their final journey – has been the way it has enhanced my sense of life, my attitude to living. No wonder the training organisation I studied with is called Living Well Dying Well. They each inform the other. They are two sides of the same coin. If you have come across works like the Tibetan Book of Living and Dying, then you will already have a clear sense of the intrinsic connection. A life well lived allows for more ease at death. A sense of our own mortality enhances our love and appreciation of life – and therefore our capacity to make good use of the days and years we have left.

A friend of mine has a cancer scare triggered by an observation during the birth of her second child. For 3 days she is worried sick and, still resting after the birth, has plenty of time to contemplate the implications. She finally admits that she hates her well paid secure job and, within a year she resigns in order to retrain as a midwife, qualifying in her early 40s. It was a tough choice but one that has transformed her and her life for the better.

"It's something everybody should go through" she says, reflecting on the gift of the cancer scare. "Of course it's horrible, but it's a real wake-up call. Faced with death I had a good hard think about my life."

Often in the final days and hours people become clearer about what really matters to them. And it tends not to be alphabetising their books or cleaning behind the bookcase. Having worked with a lot of other End of Life doulas, this list, published on Wikipedia, seems pretty consistent with what we find:

Top five regrets of the dying

- "I wish I'd had the courage to live a life true to myself, not the life others expected of me."
- "I wish I'd had the courage to express my feelings."

- "I wish I had stayed in touch with my friends."
- "I wish that I had let myself be happier."
- "I wish I hadn't worked so hard."

Maybe there are changes you could make in some of these areas while you still have the choice? Every moment brings us opportunities to feel happiness, sadness, frustration or despair. We choose the filters we apply.

Swami Sivananda the 123 year old Indian yogi described as the "oldest and happiest man in the world" says that happiness and simplicity are what keep him going.

"I had decided how to live my life in the correct way at the age of 6." Already an orphan, he chose a life of spiritual and physical exercise, healthy food, yoga and "good thoughts, good actions and good wishes".

Love, friendship, honesty… all of these can come to the fore when the end is in sight. So why not live like this starting right now?

During my training, this increased awareness of what really matters in the last stages of life caused me to reflect on how I was living my life at the time. These reflections led me to resign from jobs and responsibilities, shed possessions that did not – as queen of decluttering, Marie

Kondo says, "spark joy" - and step back from relationships or tasks that didn't feel 'on purpose' for me. Challenge the goals I was still striving for and consider instead what actually gives me happiness and fulfilment.

I realised that being able to *do* something, even do it well, wasn't the same as it being necessary or helpful for me to be doing it. For me or for the greater good. I believe that the more of us are awake and conscious about our life choices, the better we will do – both individually and collectively.

So I now choose to live more consciously, more fully… and, as a result, more joyfully. I study things I am interested in instead of those I think I *should* be interested in. I spend more time doing the things that give me peace or inspiration or satisfaction or joy, and less time on the leftover habitual behaviours and activities that had probably made sense once but had outlived their usefulness.

And most shocking of all – these days I even allow *inactivity* to play a positive role in my life. Realising the deep satisfaction that can come from an hour sitting by a stream or watching the work of the ants in my garden. This was maybe the hardest shift for me – disconnecting from that deeply engrained work ethic, seasoned with guilt. The voices in my head pronouncing me "so selfish!" or "so lazy!" took a while to settle down. But my experience has been that less is more.

I spent a beautiful five minutes over breakfast this morning watching a kingfisher, proudly strutting his stuff, all the while waiting for the perfect moment for his fast, deadly accurate dive into the fishpond to catch his lunch. He was task focussed for sure, but not to the exclusion of enjoying the moment.

As a practical example of this shift for me, some of the behaviour analysis work I do requires intense concentration. My old pattern was to slog it out. Forcing myself through page after page of analysis with the promise of a treat at the end. I have now discovered that if I do the work in 20 minute bursts – followed by a 20 minute break doing something completely different – I actually get the work done in less time overall and at a higher level. Yes! The rest / play period is as long as the concentration period. This was a counter-intuitive discovery for me and it has restored my pleasure in the work as well as improving the outcome for my clients.

Part 3: Walls in our World…The Wall of Death

It depends what kind of work you do of course – and how your supervisor feels about this approach! But in my case, all those years of pushing through were not the most effective – or pleasant - approach after all.

Part of the training for an End of Life Doula includes a rehearsal of one's own death. This may feel scary or abhorrent to you. You may find yourself shying away from an opportunity to confront this, but I highly recommend it. You can find a guided meditation to assist with this process on my YouTube channel (youtube.com/catherineshovlin). Or you may prefer to devise your own ritual and process.

There is no right or wrong way to approach this. The important thing is to walk through the wall of death. To realise that it is there and that you will face it one day. And that the first step of accepting this reality can be an enormous source of peace. It is not one jot more or less likely that you will die than it was before you did this exercise – but now it may hold less fear for you. There may be some peace around the concept that didn't exist before. And by embracing your death you may find yourself embracing your life.

Part 3: Walls in our World…The Wall of Death

When we see death as part of the circle of life, we can all live more fully, more intentionally and with more meaning. Accepting our own mortality is a compelling reason to celebrate life!

Wall of Death	
CAUSE: fear of the unknown, cultural mores, traumatic experiences, unprocessed grief	**COST:** repressed grief, unexpressed fear of death, mental and spiritual anguish, poor preparation of practicalities (no will, loose ends etc)
Walking through the wall	
CODE: allow a natural conversation about death, with others or alone. Reconnect with the cycle of life, accept the beginnings and endings	**BENEFITS:** more scope for a peaceful death for the dying party and those left behind, more ability to accept of the deaths of others in our lives

The Wall of Isolation

Although Essaouira, on Morocco's Atlantic coast, where I spend a good portion of my time these days, is a walled city; it has a spirit and history of openness that is to its credit. They say it is the only town in Morocco where you have Christian, Jewish and Muslim cemeteries and places of worship cheek by jowl. Its focus since the 1800s has been craftsmanship, taking advantage of the oceanside port to export ceramics, textiles, leatherwork, silverwork and intricate marquetry inlaid furniture to all over the world.

The majority culture is Berber, and these are a deeply hospitable and warm-hearted people, often speaking 7 or more languages and interested in everybody. Unusually they also have women leaders and warriors, and it is noticeable that the men are often out with their babies and children. In a harsh desert environment, community is paramount to survival. As Darwin actually said, it is the *most collaborative* who survive - rather different to the competitive implications of "survival of the fittest" false rumour. The Berbers live by this rule.

Part 3: Walls in our World…The Wall of Isolation

The focus of the town of Essaouira is not one of maximising shareholder value. It is about maximising joy and community.

I am sitting on a near deserted beach watching the gentle waves roll in and the plovers gathering and scattering at the shoreline. I have decided to be here for twenty minutes. A welcome change from the meditation cushion at home. As always in this part of the world a stiff breeze slaps my hair against my face, but the sun is warm.

I am just beginning to notice that the sand is feeling a little cold and damp, wondering if I will make it to twenty minutes, when a stranger taps me softly on the shoulder. My eyes flash open and my urban self is already on the alert for trouble as I whip my head round. He nods and silently offers me a blanket to sit on. Astonished, I accept it gratefully. When I turn round to see where he has come from, he is already disappearing back into the dunes. Now twenty minutes is no problem.

When I comment on this kind of everyday kindness to the Berbers, their response is always the same. They give me a slightly puzzled look and comment "It's normal". This lack of division and much reduced sense of binary existence (you? or me?) is beautiful to witness and an inspiration to us all.

It gives me cause to reflect on why we are generally not so naturally helpful towards each other in the West. It is partly shyness, especially in Britain (or perhaps that is only England). A sense that it is an implied criticism to offer help. That we should all be perfectly capable of managing on our own.

It can be fear too. If I help them what will I be getting into? Will I be responsible for them? Will I be trapped by a needy person wanting my help all the time?

I tried to set up a buddy system in my local neighbourhood a few years ago. The RSA (see thersa.org) had done a community network mapping in my neighbourhood and several others around the UK. In our little corner of London, the study revealed that there are a lot of people who feel they have nobody to turn to in times of practical or emotional need. All this loneliness and isolation seems unnecessary in a city where millions of people are crammed into a few square miles. I imagine the converted Victorian houses – 4 or 5 flats (apartments) per house now, each with one person in them. All lonely.

Or tower blocks where the only interaction is around the bins or noise complaints.

If this many people are lonely, what is the wall that is stopping them from reaching out? It would be so much easier to move that bed with some help than struggling alone. But we have created a world where it is not easy to ask, or to offer. I tried to set up the buddy system to create new protocols to start to bridge this gap. Maybe someone would appreciate a walking companion once a week, or someone to take their library books back, or bring a hammer round to bang in a nail. Maybe there was just something on a high shelf they couldn't reach. Light tasks, light connection. Not a lifelong contract of dependency, just a helping hand.

To my surprise, very few people were prepared to volunteer. They were afraid of creating dependency. Of being committed to someone and losing some freedom. Of liability. Of getting into something they couldn't get out of and would grow to resent.

Back in Essaouira meanwhile, I have just had a double mattress delivered. The motorbike rider squeezes through the narrow alleyways inside the car-free city. Without being asked, dozens of shopkeepers lean out and lift their baskets or other wares out of the way as we wind our way through. Nobody rolls their eyes or complains, they just know this is the way of things here and they get on with it.

When we arrive at the house, I explain by pointing, that the mattress needs to go up three flights of narrow stairways. The man who has got it this far is clearly committed to seeing the task to the end. Without saying a word, he nods and goes back out into the alley. Within a minute, three men I have never seen before are helping him manhandle the unwieldy burden up the building. Afterwards they nod at me as I thank them and hand out glasses of water, before they melt away back into the alleyways. The whole thing has been perfectly executed in two or three minutes.

It is not transactional. There is no money exchanged or even much need for gratitude – I express it of course but they are mildly surprised. It is just a given for them that when someone can't manage, you help them and that's that. No sense of "you owe me one" or "let me buy you a beer" or any of the other awkward ways we try to set the record straight in the UK – and, I imagine in lots of other western style countries. Fear of indebtedness snapping at our heels.

Would someone in London even want three strange men in their house? Would that make them feel vulnerable? Is that the fear which lies at the root of our resistance? Or maybe, more simply, is it the fear of being vulnerable. Of looking needy. Of not having everything Under Control. Not being On Top Of Things. Oh, how hard we may have made things for ourselves. When we could all be experiencing the simple gratitude of being helped, or the satisfying feeling of helping.

Maybe a better way to start a Buddy system would have been to start with facing isolation. Years ago, in a traditional village where everybody went to the same church, this might have been dealt with by the priest or vicar. Even in London twenty years ago, when I was still a churchgoer, the parish priest might say "Catherine have you got your car? Mrs Wilson would really appreciate a lift home". It only took me a few minutes. I felt better all day. But I would never have offered, and she would never have asked. It took Fr Pat as the middle-man to make it happen. How can we recreate that kind of common sense – a sense of having things in common - in modern times?

We have seen some signs of it during the COVID-19 period. Everybody knew that some people were isolated for health vulnerability reasons or because they had the virus. And that others were struggling to put food on the table once their zero hours contracts shuddered to a halt. Communities found ways to find out who those people were and reach out to them. The special circumstances made this "allowed". There was a sense of camaraderie and joint effort. An extended version of the situation when everybody swept the snow off the part of the pavement (sidewalk) that was in front of their house. (Before rumours of being sued for not doing it properly put people off this small act of civil duty).

In times of adversity maybe the stakes are high enough to overcome some of this social wall. We become more like the Berbers needing to help each other to survive the desert.

People are walking through this wall more often these days. The creative challenge is to find ways to stop anyone rebuilding that wall once the crisis is over.

Wall of Isolation

CAUSE: old cultural connections lost, and new ones not created. Fear of intrusion, dependency or showing vulnerability	**COST:** loneliness, isolation, poor mental and physical health, unnecessary suffering, disconnection between haves and have nots

Walking through the wall

CODE: create new protocols to forge connections between people. Build bridges and make it easy for someone to make the first move – and for another to accept it	**BENEFITS:** mutual support, friendship, improved well-being, more resilient communities

The Wall between Generations

"Let some allowance be made for youth, some freedom given to the young. Let pleasure be not always denied, and true and unbending reason not always prevail". Cicero in Pro Caelio.

I love the line in Westside Story, *"You was never my age!"*. And throughout history that has been an issue. Whichever side of the wall you are on, you know you are right and those on the other side are not only wrong, they are incapable of understanding your point of view. They don't know your world and you don't know theirs. Each party knows that they are right and everybody else is wrong.

It is natural – and important - that there is some creative tension between generations. Times keep changing, possibilities keep changing, we each have our own experiences. If you have lived through a world war or a famine or a natural disaster, of course you will have a different attitude to someone who hasn't. If you have been subjected to more rigid social conditioning than your children, then you will have different responses.

Part 3: Walls in our World…The Wall between
Generations

I arrogantly thought I was avoiding these pitfalls when I
had my own children. Right from the start I involved
them in decision making. Even as babies on the changing
mat I would hold up two outfits – they were always very
clear which one they wanted. Later, on family holidays
we would have a "Leader of the Day" badge. Whoever's
turn it was with the badge had a budget and could decide
what we did that day. If they wanted to blow it all eating
nothing but ice cream they could. If they wanted to go to
the zoo, they might choose to make sandwiches to take so
there was enough money for the entry tickets. It worked
really well. We did a wider variety of things, and
everybody knew they would have their turn soon they
had an incentive to cooperate with another child's plans. I
retained right of veto but in fact I never needed to use it -
they self-regulated perfectly. From as young as two years
old they got the concept and enjoyed the temporary
power, learning at the same time, that it was also a
responsibility.

However as they became teenagers, I realised I actually
had no idea of their inner worlds. I knew how to treat
them if they were like me. But they existed in a different
century. They lived in London and I had grown up in a
small village in the north of England. I had spent my

Part 3: Walls in our World…The Wall between Generations

childhood without internet, takeaways, text messages, gangs… their world is not my world.

As my son explained with exasperation "You walk around in your shining bubble. You're ok. You have no idea what it's like when every time you step outside the door you are seen by total strangers as a threat – without doing anything! When people look at you with fear or suspicion and not friendliness or acceptance". He is right. I have no idea what that is like.

As each of them hit puberty, we had a period of adjustment to the wall that seemed to have sprung up overnight between us. None of us knew what we were doing. My generation of parents had changed the rules about discipline and control… and now we were in uncharted waters.

"What did we do wrong?" my friends and I said to each other over and over again. "How did this happen? I thought we were going to be different."

We made the mistake of thinking the coaching that we had invested in our toddlers (manners, putting your plate in the dishwasher, sharing your feelings, hugs and

snuggles, recycling and the rest) would always be in play.
But no, here was the Generation Wall. I had the feeling at
times that both my offspring and I were gazing tragically
at it wondering where it came from, wishing it had a
doorway in it, and feeling like it would be there for ever.

It's not of course. I reckon the two most important things
for a parent of a teenager to hear are "it's not about you"
and "it's not for ever". Probably the same two things are
equally important for the teenager who is experiencing
their own struggles to find their place in the world.

There is a grieving process for both sides. The parent who
could magically make things better for a young child, is
bewildered by suddenly being unable to communicate
with the older version of that small person, let alone make
everything better.

Meanwhile the young person is yearning for freedom and
individuality – they are hard wired to break away from
their parents so they can step out into the world. And at
the same time they find themselves pitched into a world
of less comfort and less access to being comforted. That's
not an easy adjustment either. Small wonder the interest
in kitten videos and fluffy bedsocks. And the welcome

development of more hugging between friends than when
I was their age (did I ever hug a friend?).

Of course the Generation Wall also serves a purpose. If
young people just replicated their parents or carers, that
would slow down progress considerably. As well as
technical innovation we need social innovation. We need
to develop new behaviours for new times. Young people,
free of a vested interest in the status quo, are perfect for
the job. Not just on a grand scale like Greta or Malala, but
also in everyday actions and challenges to the system.

When my daughter and her friends all bought That Year's
Skirt for school, the headteacher was alarmed. It was Too
Short. Something Had To Be Done.

The senior staff try making an announcement in
assembly. But from the parents' point of view, that year's
uniform allowance has already been spent and the girls
they certainly aren't giving up something they have so
carefully chosen.

Teachers try picking them off individually. "It's not that I
mind but, you know, it's The Rules" they explain,
carefully walking the tightrope between friendly mentor
and disciplinarian. In my day that might have worked,
but these girls have been raised in homes where debate is

normal and blind obedience to church or state is not.
"Why is it the rules?" they counter.

The authorities come up with their best answer: "Because
it's always been like that". The girls counter with how
there had always been slaves until the abolitionists
challenged it. Tradition is no justification in their mind.
The democratic vote of the dead. Not valid!

"Well the boys might get the wrong idea" is the next
argument. The girls counter that, by requesting a special
assembly to educate the boys on respect and consent.

When the prefects (a common concept in British schools
where from 14 years and up, some children are selected
for these semi-authority positions) are chosen they are
told they have to change skirts to "set a good example".
Since the majority of the prefects are girls, and all but two
are wearing The Skirt, this is a risky strategy and the girls
spot that weakness immediately. Well then fire us, they
counter. The subject is parked for later discussion.

They are graded for a lot of subjects, so my daughter does
a quick survey of skirt lengths in each of the 8 maths
classes. Surprise, surprise. The highest sets have the
highest incidence of short skirts. Correlation may not be

Part 3: Walls in our World…The Wall between
Generations

causation, but the resulting graph still strengthens their
case.

"If short skirts correlate with leadership skills (chosen as
prefects) and maths ability (higher maths set), shouldn't
you be encouraging everyone to wear them?" they
suggest, tongue in cheek.

In the end the school management drops the subject.

I was deeply impressed by the way they handled the
whole six-month debate with calmness, poise and reason.
Their position – so different from their mothers'
generation – was not to *fight* for their rights, but to *identify*
them and require that the authorities justify their
decisions. They sweetly turned the tables. And my
generation had a chance to learn from the next one.

Similarly, in one of the refugee camps where I spent some
time, "youth" kept coming up as a source of discontent
for the older adults.

"They don't do anything",

"They just cause trouble"

Compared to young people in inner London they seem
pretty harmless to me, but perception is all.

Part 3: Walls in our World…The Wall between
Generations

Another factor is that the children normally in school are on their 3 month long summer holiday so are generally also swarming around the camp. At least they can have a bit of fun chasing each other but we find that we are spending way more time on entertaining the children in order to allow our programmed activities to continue, than we would normally have to do.

It dawns on me that these walls between generations aren't helping anybody. But my focus isn't on the wall between youths and adults, it is the one the youths have around themselves. They are struggling to find their identities, like young people everywhere. They are no longer allowed to hang out with any girls (unless they are married to them). They are a fairly small group and there are very few options to study, work or play.

I get them together – young men and young women at the same time which is allowed because I am chaperoning. The usual complaint of "there's nothing to do" is crushingly true in a refugee camp where they are too old for school, not allowed to work and have no leisure facilities. But that isn't their main issue. They are more concerned that they feel like outsiders in their own community. I ask if they ever feel underestimated. Hell

yeah! is not in their lexicon, but if it had been that's how
they would have responded.

I ask them if they knew how to do anything - a skill or a
talent or some knowledge - that they might be able to
teach to the younger children. They are full of ideas.
Football. Zumba. Boxing. Maths. Drumming. Sewing.
Drawing…. The list goes on. They beam with pride as
they describe their area of expertise, remembering the joy
of capability, in a world where, more often than not, they
feel useless.

We spend two hours, with the support of one of the
community organisers. By the end she has a list of ten
activities, who is going to lead each one, what age group
and gender (if applicable) the sessions will be for and
what equipment needs to be found. There is a beautiful
moment of serendipity when the community worker
remembers they have boxing equipment in the cupboard
– sent by a donor a year earlier and never even removed
from its packaging. Dots are joining up all over the place.

I hand out "Changemaker" cloth patches for them to sew
onto their clothes. A welcome recognition of their new
status. As a closing round I explain that helping others is
always an exchange and ask them what they think *they*

will gain from the experience. They identify leadership
skills, organising capacity, credibility, respect and
practising their own area of skill. But their biggest reason
is to spend more time with the little kids. To feel their joy
and love. I am deeply touched.

Would that be the same in the West if we introduced a
similar concept? Of course in the refugee camp we had
the advantage of the lack of alternative activities. No
game consoles or tablets to while away the hours. But
even so, maybe there is something in this, in the Leader
for the Day and the Youth Leader concepts.

Each one of us hungers for self-actualisation, whatever
our age or how awake we are to that need. Maybe as a
society we are missing a trick by putting a wall around
"youth" and giving it a wide berth.

Part 3: Walls in our World…The Wall between
Generations

Wall between Generations	
CAUSE: lack of self-esteem on either side, over-attachment to 'the right way ', fear of chaos, fear of judgment, unprocessed grief at the change, resistance to change	**COST:** family strife, brake on self-actualisation, waste of energy, disenchanted youth causing trouble in communities
Walking through the wall	
CODE: all generations getting over themselves and accepting more is possible, opening their hearts and minds to the possibility that the other may have value	**BENEFITS:** more harmony (not similarity) between generations, more support for all, more chances for young people to develop and grow

Part 4:
Walls in Organisations…The Wall between Generations

Part 4: Walls in our Organisations

Context

In my working life I have looked into and advised a wide range of organisations. Including government departments, schools, hospitals, NGOs, corporates, professional bodies and start-ups. They have been in five different continents and covered many styles of organisational culture. Some of those studies have involved listening to thousands of employees while others have been working with small teams.

So far, I have never come across an example of an organisation where everybody felt they knew what others were doing. Far less agreed. The concept of teamwork sometimes, though not always, exists in small groups but rarely, in my experience, beyond that. Accounts blame sales, production blame distribution, planning blames marketing… and everybody blames HR and HQ.

Of course the sample is not entirely fair. Organisations that are running smoothly, where most people are happy, and objectives are being met, don't tend to call anyone in to help. So I'm not saying this is a universal problem – only that it is extremely widespread.

Part 4:
Walls in Organisations…Context

I would love to work with a Teal organisation and see if things are different. Wikipedia describes this new approach to management as "an emerging organizational paradigm that advocates enabling employee autonomy and to adapt as an organization grows. It was introduced in 2014 by Frederic Laloux in his book on Reinventing Organizations."

For the purposes of Walking through Walls though, let's look at some examples of how and why walls show up in organisations, what harm they do both to the individual employees and to the business objectives. Importantly too, some ways crack the code and tackle them.

The Wall of Ignorance

This large multinational has called me in to identify ways they can understand and promote the concept of diversity and inclusion in their organisation. Via a series of large-scale conversations on the Synthetron.com platform I gather a massive amount of data on points of view on the topic amongst the workforce. As well as thousands of verbatim ideas and views I also have data on how widely and strongly held these points of view are.

Delving into what ends up being around a million data points, I start to see some patterns emerging. Although of course each individual has their own position, back story and preferences, there are tendencies showing up in some groups of the population.

It is all too easy with this kind of analysis to start with some assumptions and look for supporting evidence. At Synthetron they prefer a grounded theory approach, where you start swimming in the data and see what it is saying. Then challenge the hypotheses and find evidence to support them – or let them go, however reluctantly! I identify some marker statements from people involved in the study, that distinguish attitudes and beliefs, then go

Part 4:
Walls in Organisations…The Wall of Ignorance

through all the participants seeing how they have responded to these marker statements.

This gives a more natural based clustering, more like the way people at a party will tend to gradually gravitate towards those people they get on with best. It might be that all the sports fans end up together in one cluster and all the parents of teenagers in another, but the party would lose its organic charm if everyone was classified and grouped from the start.

On this ground-up basis, I consider the make-up of each of the segments defined by attitudes, looking for any tendency characteristics. Are some groups more male than others? Older on average? Whiter on average? More likely to work in an office or out in the field? And so on.

What emerges is certainly not a malign culture of repression. The classic "in-crowd" – white, male, middle aged, senior, described by some employees as the power group – are well meaning. They just have no idea how much the cultural model of the whole organisation is based on their own preferences and styles - and therefore a handicap for anybody coming from a different point of view. The power group are strong minded, successful, driven individuals. Used to working hard and playing hard. The sort of industrial man bred by years of tough schooling, competitive sports and a hierarchy that rewards the highly competitive over the thoughtful or cooperative. (Take that Darwin!)

Maybe their mothers adored them, their fathers beat them, their sports coaches humiliated them into higher performance. Maybe they have just never had to consider how their behaviour affects others because inside the walled city they have helped build, everything seems to work perfectly.

They know the rules, they know how to win and that's what they're doing. Their employers have always been happy with that. These are the guys you can send on assignment to remote and hostile corners of the planet. They'll take it on. If there is any hesitation, then the promise of a promotion on return is usually enough to tip the balance. If the wife and kids are less keen on the destination, then it just so happens that the system has invented the concept of a grass widower – let the man work in the field and look after the family in more comfortable conditions back home. He can visit every couple of months – surely that's enough to sustain a family?

Part 4:
Walls in Organisations…The Wall of Ignorance

Such is the power of the corporation and the lure of promotions and salary increases, that this situation has normalised, and families have adapted to the long-term absence of the father figure. Needless to say it is rarely the other way round though that is starting to happen more often where the mother of the children has better earning capacity and they couple are looking to maximise family income or let her have the satisfaction of a high-flying career.

These separations to do not come without a personal price. Life in a distant outpost is tough and lonely. It can be masked with beer and watching sport on TV, but it is not natural for humans to live like this for extended periods of time. Walls must be built internally to keep feelings at bay. Emotion – seen as weakness – cannot be shown. Get louder. Get rougher. Work harder. Drink harder. Pack it all away.

And when the absent parent gets home on leave, they discover a family that has learned to live without them. A friend of mine in this situation with four young children always found it challenging when Daddy came home. The children were thrilled to see him of course, but the easy rhythm of days was disrupted, and he had different disciplinary views to her. There become lots of small details about each child that it is harder to understand if you don't spend much time with them. The one that was always eating chicken is now only wanting carrot sticks, last month's favourite bedtime story is so over. Not to mention the challenge for the couple and their relationship.

It can be easier for everyone to put up some walls to cope with this family situation. If he is only home for three days do you really want to spend two of them arguing? It can be easy to decide to just put up with the things you disagree with because he'll be gone again soon. To accept a whirlwind weekend of trips to the zoo and pizza feasts then deal with the come down after he leaves by squashing away your own loneliness and disappointment and putting on a cheerful smile for the kids.

With maybe several periods like this in one's life experience, then the despising of "weak" emotions in oneself can spill over into a lack of acceptance of them in anyone else. Research into serial expatriates shows how this lifestyle has an impact on their attachments. They know they are in a place for maybe 2 or 3 years. They create a circle of acquaintances fairly efficiently, people to play tennis with or meet for drinks. But the research evidences a reluctance to bond more closely when you know that you – or they - will be moving on in the foreseeable future. Add the social risk where friends and work colleagues (competitors) are often the same people and it becomes hazardous to confide in each other. Best keep everything packed away. Behind the wall.

When I started working in the Oil and Gas industry in the early 80s, inclusion meant allowing me in the door. This was seen, and felt by me, as a significant concession. I was allowed in the building and grateful for the opportunity – despite the obvious complication of being female. The very last thing on my mind was asking for any special treatment. I was there to compete with the men, on their terms and by their criteria. To out-man the men. I didn't go so far as dark suits, I still wore colourful clothes, but I was always ready to outperform my peers. Even in small details. In those pre-mobile phone days, hotels offered a wake-up call. I would wait till all of my colleagues had specified their times (not difficult since they were quick to speak and the receptionist would tend to turn to them first). Then I would say a time ten minutes after the latest one. I wasn't giving them any quarter to make comments about how long women take to get ready! Even if it meant rushing my breakfast.

Part 4:
Walls in Organisations…The Wall of Ignorance

I flourished in that environment and made good progress up the organisation, but looking back I realise they lost out on some of the skills I could have brought to the workplace if I had been encouraged to operate in my own style.

When I set up a Women's Network in the workplace ten years later, we discovered that we all shared similar experiences in our annual appraisal meetings. We were all marked down for not being angry enough. For not shouting or thumping the table. Not being tough enough (i.e. bullying and swearing). All of us had exceeded our targets so the issue wasn't about us getting the job done. The issue was only one of style. In the process of being tough and acting tough being one of the survival criteria for working conditions involving high levels of competition, social isolation and long hours, toughness had been mistaken for the objective.

Indeed, imbued with that way of thinking, I felt a glow of pride myself when my staff in a South American country started referring to me as La Macha. I'd made it. I was super tough too. I'd fallen for the story, despite all the additional female hormones associated with being pregnant and having a small child at home. I took all the workplace call for toughness and then added being a

Part 4:
Walls in Organisations...The Wall of Ignorance

single parent with no support network. Bring it on, I can deal with anything. What was I thinking?

This is how culture operates. It takes a behaviour and rewards it until it becomes normalised. Then it inches it along the scale. Last year's extreme becomes this year's usual. New extremes develop. Armies and terrorist cells make use of this tendency to make the impossible action not only seem possible but also entirely reasonable. This same philosophical drift makes dealing with institutional racism in eg police forces, extremely challenging.

After a few years away from that context I can see the pointless heroics of going straight into the office from a 14-hour flight. But when everybody inside the city wall is doing the same thing, you can forget to notice.

In the 21st century there has been a growing realisation that diversity in the workforce is of most value when employees are also allowed to be diverse in their approaches. The more points of view the better. I might think differently to you because of my gender or my nationality. Also maybe because I am lefthanded or have travelled a lot. Maybe you are more creative or less conventional. You had different values modelled by your parents and different experiences. You are the sum of everything that has happened to you so far – the triumphs and the setbacks, the unusual hobbies and the overseas trips. The best outcome will be if we can include all that we are. No walls. No exclusions. All of my experiences and all of yours. All of my skills and all of yours.

How to change a large corporation then?

A key first step is finding agreed benefits. If you are "one of the boys" in every sense of the phrase, then why would you volunteer to yield power to others? Sometimes because legislation forces you to. But more powerfully and sustainably from realising why it's a good idea. Not to be nice to those outside the power group, not as a concession, but rather as a sign of being big enough to be open to otherness. To realise what a wonderful concoction you might make together.

Ignorance does not mean being stupid. It just means being in a state of unknowing. This is exactly what is happening in this latest organisation I started this chapter talking about. Fertile ground for that legendary unconscious bias that is found in so many aspects of our society. I also see the supporting role played by ignoring the situation. Pretending the problem isn't there or hoping it will somehow go away without too much inconvenience. Or abject terror at the thought of going into the "I don't know territory".

In the final report I enlarge on this last observation. In large organisations there is often a culture of having to know the answers. If you don't know, then bullshitting an answer is held in higher regard than saying I don't know. I notice it in social engagements with my friends who are still part of the corporate world. "It's ok to not know," I remind them when I spot the body language of the bullshitter coming into play. Ironically the times when I risked giving that answer to my superiors their response was "wow, you must be super-confident to be able to say that".

Notwithstanding, the norm is to always know the answer. That makes diversity and inclusion impossible since none of us knows what it is like to be another person – especially one coming from a very different frame of reference and values system. No matter how smart the five guys in the room are, they don't instinctively know what would motivate people who are different from themselves. That flexible working might be more valuable to an employee than a corner office. That being allowed to speak in meetings without constant interruptions or dismissal might have more impact than a pay rise.

So if you are not the person you are speaking about, and you feel you are not allowed to say you don't know what they want, you end up making uninformed decisions on their behalf that may or may not hit the mark.

The first step, I recommend to a baffled board, is to reintroduce "I don't know" into the lexicon. Followed of course by "And I'd like to find out".

However, by removing the wall of embarrassment around the topic – in this case via anonymous conversations where nobody knew the age / gender / race / seniority of anybody else in the group – people have a new way to walk through the wall. Or at least shout loud enough from their side to be heard on the other.

In this safe space, for once people can express their deeply held views, even if they are politically incorrect. They can vent their secret opinions – and maybe see them with fresh eyes in the process. Hiding the unacceptable thoughts doesn't make them go away. Better bring them out into the light and see what to do with them. Know what you are dealing with.

Part 4:
Walls in Organisations…The Wall of Ignorance

A second major advantage of an inclusive conversation is that everybody can be part of suggesting and developing solutions, even if they aren't power brokers in the everyday organisational culture. The most interesting perspectives sometimes come from the outsiders in the corporate society. Not those with seniority or influence. The security guard can know more about the sort of people who come in the store –who ends up buying and who is just there for curiosity or shelter from the rain – than the marketing department shut away in an office building on the other side of town. Tapping into the diverse thoughts and points of view of the whole workforce brings a refreshing diversity to the situation. Even of the ideas need some refinement, they can be the first step in a cascading thought process that leads the business as a whole to fresh new conclusions.

So breaking through the wall of insiders and outsiders, the power group and the rest, can disrupt the usual patterns of thinking, increasing innovation and resilience. It is also of course motivating and empowering for everybody, however unimportant they feel in the hierarchy, to be given an equal chance to have their say.

When it comes to cultural change, sometimes, before the wall can be broken down, we need to be given a chance to hop over it and see what's on the other side – not mad monsters as it turns out, but people with concerns, motivations, hopes and fears – a bit like you in fact.

So instead of just ignoring the "Others" on the far side of the wall, how about going visiting? Take a look around. Smell the roses. Experience the discomforts over there. Gain a new perspective, develop insights based on combinations of observations that you might otherwise never have experienced. Take a chance, you can always go back to your side of the wall if you don't like it!

Part 4:
Walls in Organisations…The Wall of Ignorance

Wall of Ignorance	
CAUSE: lack of awareness of other points of view which are seen as not valid, unconscious bias, early programming by schools, families and the media, prevailing culture	**COST:** organisations choosing employees or promotions from a smaller pool, less creativity, poorer health and safety record, unfulfilled employees
Walking through the wall	
CODE: honest conversations about the fears that prevent inclusion. Legitimising an approach of "I don't know… and I'd like to find out. From top management down.	**BENEFITS:** better business solutions that work for everyone, more creativity, productivity, staff loyalty and better well-being for employees

The Wall of Departmentalisation

The arts project carried out by Artmongers.org in the new children's autism wing in a major London hospital transformed the walls of the building. It also challenged the walls between different departments and professions in the hospital, testing everyone's patience in the interests of the patients.

The steering group for the ward redevelopment project was run by estates management and included people responsible for maintenance, cleaning and funding / managing the building contract. However as well as the two of us from Artmongers the team also included clinicians, the receptionist and others with direct patient contact.

It was obvious from the start that finding common ground between all these different parties wasn't going to be easy. In fact as we found out afterwards, even the tender process, involving all of these parties and more than a dozen prospective suppliers, raised controversy and dividing lines between those more focused on patients and those more focused on systems.

Part 4:
Walls in Organisations…The Wall of Departmentalisation

While there was a prevailing view of what 'art' looked like in this context, both Artmongers and the clinicians were adamant that this must be art with a purpose. That every single one of what turned out to be the fourteen artworks, every colour in the colour palette, every chair or piece of signage, was there for a reason. That it could, and should, all work together under a common creative concept with the goal of making the time in the ward less stressful and more productive for the children, their families and the specialists helping them.

We all appreciate the challenge. Patients travel sometimes 2 or 3 hours to get to the clinic for evaluation. Both parents and the ASD (autistic spectrum disorder) child arrive frazzled from the journey and stressed about the appointment. The stakes are high, the possibilities for derailment considerable.

We need to use the art pieces to smooth the experience of the whole patient and family journey. From arriving at the facility, spending time in the waiting room and moving from there to the treatment rooms. This requires everyone to look at a broader picture than they might usually. Not just the artistry but the cleanability. Not just the number of seats but the navigability. Not just the perfect solution but the affordable one.

Part 4:
Walls in Organisations…The Wall of Departmentalisation

It also requires breaking down the wall of propriety and stretching the boundaries of professional behaviour a little. Many ASD kids appreciate wordplay and witty humour and not everyone in the group finds it easy to accept there might be jokes in the art. In the end though, the patient view wins the day and we are able to create a special environment. One which allows patients to feel safe, intrigued and understood. Thereby creating space for parents to feel a little more relaxed, and, importantly, giving clinicians more scope to do their job.

Life was easier when the walls were still there. Less to think about. Simpler answers. But the solutions created that way were less powerful or less effective. It's worth the effort of breaking them down and seeing the bigger picture.

In the end, the toughest wall is often the wall between the optimistic opportunists and the pessimistic proceduralists. And that is true on this project too. The former welcome the stimulation of our weekly progress meetings, exploring ideas, bringing their own thoughts and inspirations, tussling with the challenges. Whereas the second find it all just another complication they could well do without. "Now what?" is uttered more than once

Part 4:
Walls in Organisations…The Wall of Departmentalisation

in response to the artist on our team when he says excitedly "I've had another idea!!"

And I sympathise of course. It is a lot to manage the practical, legal, budgetary and medical aspects of a hospital. Compared to a lot of the heavy processes they were involved with in their day to day work, this art business must seem at times to be unbearably lightweight and inconsequential. But we know from impact research that it *does* make a difference. That subtle touches like the gleaming opalescent isobars flowing down the corridor which help patients make the sometimes difficult 20 metre journey from the waiting room to the treatment room, are worth all of the effort involved in agreeing and creating them.

Understanding how to approach the project requires us to step through the wall between the neurotypical and those on the spectrum. We read, we watch documentaries, I attend the 3-day National Autism Conference and meet many individuals and their families. I learn for example how the colour red can be a hook for some people with ASD. It distracts them and they can't stop looking at it. This makes me think how, with my colour psychology hat on, I *know* that red is the colour that is seen first and fastest. So to some extent we all have this tendency, but

Part 4:
Walls in Organisations…The Wall of Departmentalisation

most of us can choose to over-ride it. To have the instinctive response to see red first and then still be able to look at other things. One young man I met had his life transformed when he got a pair of glasses that filtered out red. Suddenly, he could get on with things without being transfixed by any red in the environment. So that's one colour that definitely is not going to feature.

We start to develop an appropriate colour palette of gentle calming colours. A far cry from the lively general children's unit elsewhere in the hospital full of vibrant primaries. Fun for a neurotypical child with a broken arm but exhaustingly over-stimulating for someone on the spectrum.

We learn about shapes too as we step through to the other side of the wall. From Temple Grandin's work with animals we learn how important curves are to allow progress. See her great TED talk (https://www.youtube.com/watch?v=fn_9f5x0f1Q) or watch the movie Temple Grandin, for more information if you are interested in the value of visual thinking and daring to be different.

Her work shows how curves and some vision of the way ahead reduce anxiety and improve livestock happiness.

Part 4:
Walls in Organisations…The Wall of Departmentalisation

We are animals too. Sharp corners are unpleasant, they
are not organic. Consider the different feel of a round
room compared to one full of sharp edges. The latter is
very stylish, but not so easy to live with. We might put
rubber corners on furniture to protect toddlers but how
many of us as adults have also suffered cuts and bruises
from inadvertent collisions with our furniture?

These issues of colour and shape are dramatically more
problematic for children on the autistic spectrum, but
there are lessons here for all of us. Do any of us want to
feel stressed by our environment? Is that bright red wall
in your bedroom helping you get a good night's sleep?
Are those gleaming hard surfaces making you feel at
home? I doubt it. But we have all fallen for the style story
and can be tempted to furnish our homes for the look
rather than the feel.

When I first saw Oasis's oval cot (crib) I couldn't believe
we had spent all these years with rectangular ones. What
purpose do those corners serve? A place for toys to get
stuck, another corner for us to collide with – there are no
corners in the womb or when you are held in someone's
arms. They maybe make sense if you are making a cot
from planks of wood several hundred years ago, but with

Part 4:
Walls in Organisations…The Wall of Departmentalisation

today's manufacturing possibilities – or some carpentry craftmanship – straight edges don't have to be the default.

We go for curves in our pans and mixing bowls, in our paint pots, in our bodies – so let's recognise the advantages elsewhere too. In office buildings, in hospitals, in schools.

As well as shapes and colours, our explorations on the other side of the ASD wall help us understand some of the differences between children on the spectrum. It is far from a single situation. We find a theme (wind) that can span from detailed maps and scientific information, to the simple visceral pleasure of wind in our hair. Our aim is to provide sufficient visual stimulus in the waiting area to keep the 4 year old as well as the 15 year old interested while they waited for their appointment. And then to facilitate the transition from waiting room to therapy room with our treatment of the corridors and doorways.

Soon after identifying the theme, I am on a family holiday thousands of miles away. An adolescent boy I don't know sits next to me while I wait for the gym to open. We start to chat and I quickly realise he is on the spectrum – a fact he proudly volunteers.

Part 4:
Walls in Organisations…The Wall of Departmentalisation

"Do you know what my favourite thing is?" he asks me. As I shake my head, he loudly announces "The wind!" I am thrilled. We seem to have hit the right track. Travelling to the other side of the wall with compassion and curiosity enables magic to take place.

In another Artmongers project in a residential facility for adolescents with severe mental health conditions, staff report that the journey up two flights of stairs from the sleeping accommodation to the art and teaching rooms sometimes takes over an hour.

We make that a priority in the project and the installation of an artwork winding up the stairs makes the transition much more manageable for the staff. It creates an intriguing experience, a talking point, a reason to progress, which the previous standard institutional staircase had not been able to deliver.

It is not easy to consider multiple points of view. There is a simplicity about staying inside your walls and optimising on your most important measures, in isolation from the rest of the system. When a dentist told my six-year old daughter to eat more crisps, they were considering only the avoidance of sugar, and not the effect on the whole body. (Luckily, she was smart enough to consider their advice holistically and decided her weekly sweets were not the problem).

Thinking about everything all of the time is of course more effort. There are more challenging compromises and trade-offs. But there is also the opportunity to generate much more satisfying outcomes. This inclusive approach encourages innovation and creative thinking in teams. Working together does not need to mean finding the lowest common denominator. It can mean finding an extraordinary new solution which only came about because the janitor sat at the same table as the chief of surgery, or the security guard shared their observations with the marketing department.

The fact that this approach also gives each party renewed understanding of and respect for what goes on in other parts of the organisation is all to the good. Fewer walls means more fluidity. More transparency. Less division and more connection. Better for the individual and better for the organisation's objectives.

Part 4:
Walls in Organisations…The Wall of Departmentalisation

Wall of Departmentalisation	
CAUSE: tough targets per department which shifts focus to smaller worlds and smaller decisions. "Us" vs "them" culture. No time to understand the other, seen as irrelevant activity.	**COST:** sub-optimal solutions for whole business despite optimal solutions for each part.
Walking through the wall	
CODE: build in time, support and processes to enhance mutual understanding and reduce internal competition so focus can be on external client or the end goals of the overall organisation	**BENEFITS:** less waste, less conflict, less energy squandered on internal disputes, more joined up thinking

The Wall of Jargon

"I think we need to develop a flick flack" I say solemnly.

"Ah yes," replies my boss. In fact my boss's boss. Templing his fingers thoughtfully and ignoring the tiny beads of sweat on his face as he nods his large sandy haired head. I watch curiously to see if they will fly off, but they stay put. "Good idea."

As I leave his dull, stuffy office I felt a bit guilty at my mischief making. I am *so* bored in this holiday job, working in the research lab of a government department. The money is good, and it is kind of amusing to go to "the office" every day – I feel like a pretend grown up. But the civil service is no place for a 19 year old and there seems to be very little to do.

The project they scheduled for me only took 3 of the 12 weeks I am here for. And I have asked every single one of the 32 engineers in the department if there is anything I can do to help. One guy says his plants needed watering while he was on holiday, but nobody else has any ideas.

My boss comes into my private office (this is pre-open plan era) and I guiltily put down the novel I brought in

Part 4:
Walls in Organisations…The Wall of Jargon

with me today. The last three days I have fallen asleep in the afternoon and reading seems slightly less sinful.

"Oh sorry, you're busy," he apologises. "I'll come back later."

"Mike, I'm reading a novel! Please give me some work."

"Oh, well, if you're sure. OK. The boss is wondering about installing flick flacks in the computer room. I heard him talking about it on the phone to the higher ups. You don't know anything about them, do you? I've no idea."

I flounder. Part proud at the rapid acceptance of my idea and part ashamed that I just made it up on the spot because I guessed – rightly it seems – that the head of the computer department knows next to nothing about computers.

I offer to ask around (no internet or I'd have been rumbled immediately) and see what I can find out. Maybe they'll forget about it before I finish. At lunchtime my fellow intern and I can hardly eat our sandwiches for giggling.

In this case my use of jargon was partly curiosity to see if I could get away with it, and partly just boredom. In many situations it is used much more intentionally as a wall to make it clear to people that they are the outsiders. I found it frustrating when I was learning anatomy (why can't they just call it the second finger bone?).

In the corporate world I was admonished more than once for writing too clearly. "It doesn't sound clever enough if people can understand it" and, according to Émilie du Châtelet, the French mathematician who translated Newton's famous work Principia Mathematica, it was originally in Latin because Newton felt the information was too important for all and sundry to know. An extended version of using jargon as a wall to make sure some people feel stupid or uneducated, and excluded.

The jargon wall is very effective to distinguish between the in-crowd and the outsiders. As any of us who have started a new job know, there's quite enough to learn at the start of a new job (everybody's names, the way to the toilet, what happens at lunch, who to watch out for… and that's before even getting started on what the business is and what the job requires). It only makes it harder if there is a lot of unnecessary jargon and acronyms.

The origin is probably pretty primitive. While the tribe works out whether or not to trust the new arrival, they need to lay a few traps to test them. Those can also be

Part 4:
Walls in Organisations…The Wall of Jargon

physical traps – sending the new apprentice to buy a tin of spotted paint, or initiation rites that can exist in boarding schools, police forces or pretty much any place where humans gather.

For a few years I was in a job which meant I had sales managers in several other countries. Vlado in Croatia is old school, 30 years older than me and an engineer. He is baffled as to why this girl is now his boss and he puts me through my paces. On each of my quarterly visits we go and visit customers, mostly to persuade them to pay their bills. This means some overnighting around the country. These are the early days after the break-up of the former Yugoslavia and the country is still in turmoil. A long time before it became a popular tourist destination. I am amazed to discover how beautiful it is. A staggering coastline, craggy mountains, fresh sea food. A delightful surprise.

The first test is drinking. I keep pace as he knocks back local wine and the next morning I appear for breakfast bright eyed and bushy tailed. He doesn't need to know I have some yoga moves up my sleeve to help with detoxing.

Part 4:
Walls in Organisations…The Wall of Jargon

"Harrumph." He greets me, Looking even craggier than usual. But cannot keep the admiration out of his voice as he observes "Good drinker."

I naively think that will be it, but the next visit requires a visit to the bowling alley. Where I managed to lose but not disgracefully. And even let him offer advice to improve my technique. Apparently, I get a pass on that one too.

Next time, we are driving from the capital, Zagreb down to Split on the coast to visit some shipping companies. After about an hour on the twisty rocky roads he stops the car.

"You drive," he says gruffly, tossing me the keys.

Eventually Vlado ran out of tests. We were chalk and cheese, but he had to admit I was true to my word and knew how to get things done. A grudging respect developed between us and by the end of the stint we had a pretty smooth good cop bad cop routine in place, allowing him to appear to be on his customers side but still getting the money they owed us because "she" is coming from head office.

Part 4:
Walls in Organisations…The Wall of Jargon

One of the insidious problems with jargon is how quickly it becomes normal to the people who know it. When I do research in hospitals about the patient experience, the hospital staff are amazed when I evidence how patients and their families don't understand the terminology. Now I am learning Indonesian I am impressed that they have straightforward and clear terms like "Children's Doctor" and "Eye Expert". Nobody needs to know what a paediatrician or ophthalmologist are.

A second challenge is that we have made it hard to not know. Like the boss at the beginning of this chapter, most people do not like to say "What does that mean?" or "I don't know". So misunderstandings can develop and future problems be generated.

Try googling "The trouble with experts" and you will find a whole wealth of material. It's not that they are trying to mislead, but if they use jargon, specialist knowledge and other behaviours to build high walls around their specialty then it is easier for common sense and holistic thinking to be included in their thinking.

Next time any of us find ourselves using jargon, we might wonder if it's simply a convenience, or if it's another brick in the wall to satisfy our ego or makes us feel more

Part 4:
Walls in Organisations...The Wall of Jargon

powerful. Creating a higher wall that might get in the way of our common progress, common sense and shared evolutionary journey.

Part 4:
Walls in Organisations...The Wall of Jargon

Wall of Jargon	
CAUSE: lack of self-esteem, need to feel better by making others feel worse, wish to belong	**COST:** some feel excluded so ideas and motivation can be lost, less transparency
Walking through the wall	
CODE: challenge jargon. Is it performing a useful job? (sometimes true) or is it about exclusion and barriers?	**BENEFITS:** everybody can be part of the discussion, more transparency / honesty

Part 4:
Walls in Organisations…The Wall of Protocol

The Wall of Protocol

The Breakfast Club and After School club at our local primary school is essential in an area where both parents often work full time or children are part of a single parent family. Secure and right on the school premises it creates a safe, friendly space where children can play, learn and create together. For those coming from busy households, the meals provided at breakfast and teatime, plus homework support, can also improve their outcomes at school.

I got involved when my own children were attending the club and I wanted to understand more about it. I discovered the management meetings were open to anyone and went along.

I am a little surprised to see that the management team are all male and all white. And that the meeting is rather more formal than I had expected. At the time I am working in the corporate world, so I'm not daunted by the familiarity – it just seems a bit unnecessary. Verging on pompous.

Part 4:
Walls in Organisations...The Wall of Protocol

I am even more surprised when, by the end of the meeting, the whole committee has faced a vote of no confidence from the staff and resigned. Suddenly I find myself hurtled from complete novice to number one candidate to take over - all in the space of a couple of hours.

I don't mind making a contribution, but I am on unknown territory here. I have children but I know little about educational or social needs of children on a wider basis. If this is going to work, I will need some support. And I want it from a group of people that better represents the families using the club.

At the Emergency Parents' meeting called to explain the situation with the board, I ask for volunteers to join me on the committee. There is a worrying silence as most people look at their feet or gaze into the middle distance.

Afterwards over cups of tea I try to find out more. Just the word "committee" is a problem I realise. From the get-go that sounds like boring hard work for clever people or someone needing it on their CV. So first decision, let's call it the Leadership. Remember you are all leaders, I remind them. You don't have to be a senior manager in a big company to be a leader. You're a leader every time you take the lead. In your family, at the pub, on a train, in your community. You're parents so you are already leaders. It goes with the territory. So you are totally qualified to be in the Leadership group. Still not a rush of volunteers.

I speak to one of the mothers who doesn't want to get involved because she has never been on a committee and so is afraid she won't know what to do and will be in trouble or look stupid. She assumes there will be a lot of procedures and correct ways of behaving that she doesn't know about – and none of us likes that feeling of being out of our depth. I note how this wall of protocol – or perceived protocol - is keeping them out.

Another explains to me that as a single-parent she can't afford a babysitter while she goes out for a 7pm-9pm meeting once a month. It is enough of a challenge to leave work in time to get to the club by close at 6pm, get everyone home and any homework or preparation jobs done – then bath-time, bedtime, feeding herself, collapsing into bed ready for the next day to roll around.

Making ends meet is the priority and a babysitter is an occasional luxury reserved for a special treat. Again, I

Part 4:
Walls in Organisations…The Wall of Protocol

take note of this wall that is stopping people from getting involved.

Another parent shares that because the meetings tend to rotate around the spacious houses of middle-class committee members complete with tasty snacks and a glass of good wine, she feels ashamed of her tiny, crowded flat. There aren't even enough places for everyone to sit down, she explains. And the kids would be shouting for the TV. So she doesn't dare to join the committee because of the social awkwardness of being the one who never hosts a meeting. And there it is, yet another wall preventing participation.

To some extent these are all accidental walls. Nobody built them with the express intention of excluding these parents. Like the unconscious bias discussed earlier, it is ignorance more than malintent. But as the Anti-Racism movement has taught us, it is not enough to be blind to prejudice. We need to be much more awake than that. On the look-out for these accidental walls we create – and then wonder why the only people who want to join in are people like us, while insisting that everyone is welcome.

The fourth wall I discover in this situation is about self-confidence. Those who feel sure they have nothing useful to contribute. "What do I know about those things?" they would ask. So I describe one or two challenges I know the committee has faced in the recent past – a personality clash between members of staff, a parent persistently collecting late so staff couldn't go home, fears about abuse at home. And of course they have views and ideas about any of these situations. Views based on the lives they have lived, the neighbours and family they know, and the challenges they have faced.

A tiny bit of the job is legal stuff and budgets, I explain. I can take care of that if you want - or teach you how to do it. But most of it is human nature. The stuff you have dealt with every day of your life. Really? Many of them are braver and tougher than me. They have certainly all had experiences that I haven't. Together our pool of experience is richer and more varied than any one of us on our own. I can honestly say to each one of them "I need your wisdom".

The fifth wall is between the committee and the staff. Under the excuse of confidentiality, staff are not invited to meetings. Instead, committee members who have never worked in the club come up with decisions that define the way the club is run. By the staff who are not involved in

Part 4:
Walls in Organisations…The Wall of Protocol

the decision. Sometimes these ideas are useful, other times they are impractical, irritating or just plain stupid.

In my view there is never a need for a small number of leaders to sit behind closed doors and magically know all the answers. We have seen during the COVID-19 pandemic how those national leaders who choose to be open and transparent: crowdsourcing solutions and involving everyone in data collection and disease management, are having way better outcomes than countries with a high Pomposity Score (by which I mean places where the leaders feel their job is to know what's best for everyone. And if they don't know they should act like they do, bullshit their way through and hope they don't get caught out.

So we take a wrecking ball to that wall too.

Armed with this better understanding we decide to make some changes to how "the committee" – now the "Leadership" - is organised.

First off – walk through the wall of protocol that is causing resistance. Together with my wary group of volunteers, we decide that all the meetings will take place in the school. At a picnic table in the playground when it is sunny, or in the club itself when it is dark or cold.

Part 4:
Walls in Organisations…The Wall of Protocol

Meetings will start earlier, at 6pm (pick up time from the club) and the Club will pay for a member of staff to stay on to look after any of the children of people at the meeting. They will already have had supper in the club but in this extra time the staff can help them get homework done – or just have fun.

All staff are welcome to come along to meetings except when any sensitive topics are being discussed (eg a disciplinary or performance related issue) which makes this inappropriate. Usually even in these situations they can be there for most of the meeting and then leave before the last, confidential part.

All communication will be on paper, delivered to people's homes as this is at a time before common possession of a mobile phone or email address – another way people are feeling they are not eligible to join.

Later, we realise this open invitation is not a good enough approach as they still felt shy about coming along. So instead we keep that offer open and also agree with the manager for one member of staff to come each time to showcase something about their work, a situation with a child or family or a new idea they feel is worth trying out.

Part 4:
Walls in Organisations...The Wall of Protocol

This helps increase our understanding of how the club operates as well as giving us a chance to celebrate a member of staff each meeting and give them a sense of being seen and heard. The flip side is having each member of the Leadership attend a session in the club from time to time to help out and see the lived experience of the staff and the children.

And most importantly of all, official procedures are kept to an absolute minimum and always explained. It is important to create an atmosphere where anyone can say "I don't know what you mean" without feeling awkward or stupid. We resolve to eat cake at meetings and enjoy each other's company as well as sort out the business of the club!

Thanks to these and other changes we introduce by collaborating together, for my four years of involvement I enjoy the teamwork of a lively, diverse and committed group of parents and staff and the club blossoms.

Like the unconscious bias I mentioned earlier, the original committee had not meant to exclude anybody. They just hadn't seen what things looked like from the other side of the wall and we had to make a conscious choice to fix that

Part 4:
Walls in Organisations…The Wall of Protocol

so that we all knew about each other's point of view in order to have the best possible system and culture.

So much of the protocol I come across is vestigial. It made sense once and nobody has reviewed it. Instead things just get added over time, so processes tend to get more and more heavy. It takes some energy to challenge and revise them, but the rewards can be huge.

Part 4:
Walls in Organisations...The Wall of Protocol

Wall of Protocol	
CAUSE: unconscious bias, assuming everyone is 'like me', laziness, conformity, bossy chair who nobody can challenge	**COST:** disengaged members, shortage of volunteers, uneven solutions that don't work for all
Walking through the wall	
CODE: ask for and understand others' points of view, identify the barriers together, be creative and open minded in finding solutions, no sacred cows.	**BENEFITS:** updated protocols that work for the people involved, improve inclusion and diversity and therefore improve solutions

The Wall of Principles

1989, the last days of Mengistu's regime – one considered to be a key factor in the 1.2 million deaths from the famine in Ethiopia from 1983 to 1985. A devastated country still reeling from famine, war and misgovernance.

The Hilton hotel is allegedly the most profitable in the group because of the endless stream of journalists and UN / aid workers on expenses. I quickly transfer to a local hotel, away from the sea of khaki pants and braying voices.

The NGO I am running during that sabbatical year from my corporate career (EthiopiAid.org) is trying to look forward with the local people. Not just focus on survival but build a better future. We are involved in supporting various locally run projects to improve health education, sanitation, income generation and child development.

In the capital, Addis Ababa, at the time, thousands of people are living in appalling slum conditions. I meet a woman who lives in a 4 square metre 'house' with her 7 children. A few slats of wood leaning together, a pile of dirty rags for sleeping on and almost nothing else. This is by no means unusual. Children run through the mud, drinking from the gutter and swatting away the flies.

One of the many issues is disease control in such an unhygienic environment, hence our contribution of a 'sludge gulper'. This is a small truck that moves around the slum area collecting sewage. A little less opportunity for disease to spread. This action is supported by training young girls in the community to spread the word about the importance of hand washing, segregated food storage and so on.

Elsewhere we are involved with slum redevelopment. Using concrete to create more weatherproof and hygienic houses.

Under the Mengistu regime, concrete production is state-managed. Supply is very limited and the queueing system is open to abuse. As an NGO with fairly small requirements we are constantly halting construction because of lack of materials.

I am aware that this problem is shared by other NGOs, so I arrange a series of meetings with the big international players – you know the names. At the first meeting I share what we are doing and in turn, they tell me about their projects. They agree that cement is a problem, both

Part 4:
Walls in Organisations…The Wall of Principles

securing supply and getting a fair price. How about we form a buying consortium? I suggest. If we all add together our requirements it will be a much more attractive order for the cement company and we should end up with a better price and more chance of getting what we need.

It seems really clear to me that this is a good idea, so I am somewhat taken aback when the apparently reasonable project manager leans over their rickety Formica desk in their sweltering office and says to me

"Yes but we have different priorities".

"Er. Yes. Of course, and I'm not suggesting you change what you do or why you do it at all. Just that we make our lives a bit easier".

"No I don't think so"

I am still baffled by his response but maybe he is just particularly narrow minded. I move on to the next meeting, thankful that I have someone who knows the city to help me travel around. I haven't seen any signposts or road names – and even if I did, the Amharic script would have meant little to me.

Part 4:
Walls in Organisations…The Wall of Principles

By the end of the day I have met with 5 international NGOs. They all say the same thing. Nobody seems to recognise this as a pragmatic solution to a practical barrier to the progress of their projects. Rather they all see it as a threat to their charitable purpose. Personally, I see it as a waste of donor's money to pay over the odds for building materials, and a deeply unfair treatment of the people we are trying to help to tell them of delay after delay to provision of habitable housing. Some of them don't live long enough to see the benefit.

In this case the wall was described as being one of principle. Even though they could not identify any way in which my suggestion undermined any of their principles. Many years later I can see that this description was the paint on the wall, not the wall itself. The real bricks in the way were based on fear of losing some control, fear of change and fear of suggesting something different in a sector structured more around developing projects (and therefore a license to operate and therefore a job) than the interests of recipients themselves.

Principles and values absolutely matter. I always urge new organisations – commercial or social – to establish those very early on. I believe they are one of the most critical things for people in a group to be aligned on. Even more than purpose because the objectives of the organisation may change over time as the needs / market / context change. But the values or principles always hold good. So long as they come with clarity and transparency. A self-confidence and understanding within the organisation of what really matters rather than a knee jerk rejection of anything that might be a threat. Lived principles which inform wise choices rather than restrictions which limit imagination and pragmatic decisions.

If you work for an organisation, you may sometimes be in situations where it is easier to say no than work out ways to say yes. Easier to be inflexible than adapt and incorporate new information or opportunities. Easier to keep your head down and stay on the same track. In these situations, I urge you to look up, maybe peep over the wall, and at least run a thought experiment of what it would mean to try something different. You may just change things for the better.

Part 4:
Walls in Organisations…The Wall of Principles

Wall of Principles	
CAUSE: competition between NGOs or social organisations, lack of autonomy of staff on the ground, confusion between principles and processes, fear	**COST:** solutions take longer to deliver to recipients, so there is more suffering while they wait, easy triumphs over great
Walking through the wall	
CODE: distinguish between principles and practicalities or processes. Ensure everyone understands the spirit of the law, not just the applications so it is possible to safeguard the organisation's ethics while optimising delivery	**BENEFITS:** lower supply costs so more can get done (better use of donors' money), fewer delays so more progress, more innovation, more collaboration

Part 5: Walls in our hearts and minds…The Wall of Principles

...

Part 5: Walls in our hearts and Minds

Context

Now, let's look at some of the most challenging walls – the ones within ourselves. Maybe your professional persona is very different to your off-duty self. Maybe you erect Chinese walls in your head to separate your view that a particular behaviour is unacceptable from the times when you have gone along with it. Maybe you are inside the wall of who you think you should be (or parents, teachers, peers or society think you should be) rather than expanding into your true self.

Identifying our own internal walls can be deeply uncomfortable. It requires courage and brings risks – and rewards of course. Making changes may be inconvenient or painful. My own view is that we each owe it to ourselves, and to our families and the wider world, to be the best that we can be. Sometimes that means challenging our own view of ourselves or recognising that having a difficult conversation or making a bold move is necessary if we are to walk through the wall.

Feel the fear

As a part-time property developer there are times when I feel the need to knock down some of the walls inside houses.

That second before the sledgehammer hits the wall is rich ground for self-doubt. Time for a deep breath and a leap of faith. Accepting the risk that it could be a horrible mistake but doing it anyway. Because with a building project – or some situations - there is no other way to find out what happens when you walk through the wall unless you just do it.

And then, a moment later, as the light from the next room streams in through the new connected whole, and the space immediately feels invigorated, I know it has been the right decision and I remember that it is exhilarating to walk through walls.

Be aware

It can help to think first of course. To consider the implications. I'm not suggesting running recklessly headlong into every wall you encounter. But I do believe there is a lot more scope for this than we remember in our day to day lives. We can get so used to the walls we live with, live behind, live within, that we can stop seeing them.

So wherever you can make the choice, open your eyes, look at the wall with an open heart and open mind. Be true to yourself. Breaking down the walls inside your own head will allow your thoughts to flow more freely, to cross-pollinate more productively. Your heart and mind can work in closer harmony, and your own particular gifts and creativity can shine brighter in the world.

Of course I have had my share of walls to face. And still do. It is an ongoing process. If you walk through a wall you may find yourself in a new space with more walls to consider. This is our story, our journey. At one point may we be stopped by the walls and accept the status quo, settle for things as they are. The walls may feel too high, too impregnable.

Some people have heroic appetites for walking through walls and continue to do so till their dying breath. Others of us may get worn down by the struggle or face some unspeakable traumas and not feel able to continue.

Sometimes we just need to take a break. To rest and restore. It is so important to take this time. Constantly walking through walls can be exciting – and it also takes its toll. Some time-out to recuperate now and then is better than getting burnt out. Maybe your journey is about many small walls, maybe it is your life's work to deal with one massive one. Do what is right for you. What calls you, what draws your attention, what enrages you, what thrills you, what intrigues you when you think about life without that wall.

Above all I hope you are aware of the walls in your own life. The ones you have walked through and the ones you have chosen to live with. Just being aware of these choices helps us distinguish. Are we done? Are we still in the process? Where is our next priority? What view do we want to open up?

In this example of a personal wall I have faced, things could have gone horribly wrong. I did take a risk at a stage in my career when the consequences would have been hard. But I like to think it removed a few bricks in this particular wall, for the good of all.

The gender wall

I am lucky enough to have grown up in a part of the world and at a time in history when the barriers to women and between gender identities and sexuality are beginning to dissolve. If I look back to the 1970s, I am astonished at the contrast. So much has shifted.

Of course I know there is still work to do. I know there is still extensive prejudice and bias. But compared to 50 years ago, or a 100 years ago, mighty strides have been made. The fact that they slip back during stressful times is disheartening, but not the same as going back to the past. The genie will not go back in the bottle. Once people have experienced freedom, they have less tolerance for losing it.

I am lucky too that I had a grandmother whose motto was "there's no such word as can't". She had 5 children and 14 grandchildren and managed those, plus the local community centre, the Girl Guides and anyone else who crossed her path with unwavering authority. If she had been born at a different time, I am sure she could have become a capable CEO. School holidays spent with her were like a skills camp. Calligraphy, woodwork, gardening, craft making, badminton, poetry writing, piano playing (probably the least successful in my case!), tree identification, crosswords and so on.

Looking back I can appreciate why – she often had half a dozen grandchildren to stay for a few weeks while their parents were working through most of the long summer holiday. She and my grandfather would take us all off in their small caravan to the seaside or a campsite in the countryside. It would be a case of all hands on deck for making camp and then the rota would be pinned up. The rota was non-negotiable.

These were low budget holidays, so we didn't spend the time visiting zoos and theme parks. I see now how important all those activities she initiated were to keep everyone occupied. In retrospect, I see too how there were no exceptions made for gender. The assumption was that everybody could do everything. There's no such word as can't.

Add to that a home where both parents worked and seemed to make decisions between them and a mixed school where it was easy to beat the boys in end of year exams, then a university degree in maths and computer science at a time when more females than males studied those subjects, and I see now why I hit the working world assuming there was no issue.

I was a little surprised to be the only female in that year's intake (1984), and to discover there was only one the year before too. I was amused to hear that they had only just dropped the "no trousers" rule for women. But I didn't actually even consider my gender would be a barrier to progress. Looking back I think that innocence was a great help, it allowed me a confidence and expectation that stood me in good stead.

A couple of months in, I am on a training course with the rest of my intake to hone our negotiating skills, I notice that the trainer keeps suggesting I sit out of the "tougher" negotiations. He doesn't exactly say sit and do your embroidery but that is the sense of it. That it could get nasty and be "too much' for me. I am sure he feels that he is being gallant. I try insisting I'll be fine. My fellow students laugh aloud at the idea that I need protecting. But he stands firm. After two days of this I decide that action is needed and arrive the next morning in a suit and tie borrowed from one of the guys, hair slicked back and sporting an elegant pencil moustache.

The trainer strides in with his usual boisterous enthusiasm and scans the room. "Good morning gentleman!" he booms as usual. "And lady!" he adds with his usual show of gracious consideration, scanning the room for me.

When he first sees me, he does a double take, and looks amused. But almost immediately something else kicks in and he looks worried. Then puzzled. Then afraid. I watch as a range of emotions travel across his face. Outrage at the insubordination. Worry at the implications. Desperately he looked at his fellow males around the room, hoping for some camaraderie. But of course they are all in on the game and all support me in my objective. They look back impassively as though puzzled about what could be at issue.

In the end he opts for completely ignoring the situation. When there's an elephant in the room, best pretend there isn't! But later when he says "only the gents for this exercise" we watch it dawn on him. Flustered and apologetic he tries to explain himself, how he is just looking out for me. Doesn't want me to get upset. I gently observe that it might be more useful for me to know how to deal with the tough negotiations I was as likely to face as my male colleagues. And that his alleged concern translates into weakening my position and increasing my vulnerability. He is still hesitant and clearly very uncomfortable. But he does reluctantly allow me to participate. Needless to say I give as good as I get and enjoy also weaving in some of my more feminine aspect skills like building rapport and a sense of shared goals in order to achieve the objectives with less conflict.

Postscript: the company recognised that some people are too well established in their patterns to welcome change and the trainer was subsequently released into early retirement. I never formally complained about his behaviour, but of course this story told itself and forced the conversation between the individual and his line manager. There's more than one way to walk through a wall! Sometimes a little wry humour can say more than a great deal of exasperated protest.

The Wall of Dis-Integrity

Nowadays we tend to think of integrity as something related to honour, morality, trustworthiness. Its original sense is wholeness. To be a person with integrity, we bring our whole selves to any situation. We don't carve up into work self, home self, party self etc. When someone is living a double life say, or acting a role that is not the natural way of being, there is a psychic cost to this schism.

We understand the term to disintegrate. To fall apart into parts or collapse. This is the sense in which I am talking here about integrity and dis-integrity.

Let me share an example of when I was living without integrity. First though, a little context...

Who among us can be sure about reality? There's the obvious sort, the table my laptop is resting on as I type, the amazing Bali view in front of me. But then if I was dreaming this would seem every bit as real and it would only exist in my imagination.

At least that is the generally accepted situation. You may feel differently. These are interesting times and the number of people considering so-called paranormal forces and events as part of our world is increasing. This along with development in quantum physics and the increasing recognition that everything is energy opens up the possibilities.

If someone hears voices, are they suffering from a mental health problem or are they a psychic? A victim or a visionary? If someone's cancer suddenly disappears without medical treatment is it a miracle or a fluke? If you think about someone you lost touch with twenty years ago and then an hour later they contact you, is that an astonishing coincidence or is something else at play?

We all have our views but since nobody absolutely definitely KNOWS for sure, I like to stay openminded. I have seen in my End of Life Doula work how faith can help someone face the uncertainty of death. Who am I to deny them that comfort? Who am I to say they are wrong even if their faith is not something I personally relate to?

For many years when I was working in the corporate world whilst exploring meditation, journeying, channelling and healing, I kept a big high wall between the two. I felt strongly that "that kind of thing" getting out would damage my corporate reputation, undermine my intellectual capacity, make me seem flaky to most of my colleagues. So I went to my workshops at the weekends, read the books at home and stuck to the rationality script in the workplace.

This was my lack of integrity, my lack of wholeness, the split in my personality. I was not a fully integrated person as I led this split life. That dis-integrity carried a personal cost. And as time went on it became unsustainable…

I don't know who is more surprised by my words to Dario, the Chief Financial Officer (CFO) during our board meeting. I glance up at the Andes in the distance for geological reassurance. For a sense of a bigger context. Our Chief Executive (CEO) at the time is a successful tyrant. An old school bully boy of significant physical stature, strong charisma, a quick mind and a taste for manipulation and absolute power.

Dario arrives a few minutes late for the meeting. Flustered and apologising, explaining he has been at the doctors. "Everything alright?" inquires the boss – pretty much a rhetorical question as mental or physical weakness is not an option in the workplace. "It's just a liver problem, but I'm fine" mutters the CFO.

Part 5: Walls in our hearts and minds…The Wall of Dis-Integrity

I look up, taking in his energy and before I know it, I hear my voice saying "You should go home Dario, your aura looks terrible. You need to rest."

Silence falls. Six perfectly groomed corporate heads look up in astonishment then flick their ties nervously and look back down at their notepads to duck whatever is coming next. I try in vain to become invisible.

The CEO looks at me. In the whole three years I have worked for him it is the only time he drops his guard. He looks exposed, cornered, caught out. Just for a second. Then he recovers quickly and starts issuing orders in his best booming baritone, so it seems like Dario is only ushered out of the room by a puzzled PA on the boss's command.

I know I have done something irreparable. I flick a cautious glance at the CEO, but he is rustling papers and launching into the agenda. He has decided to deal with my unexpected comment by ignoring it.

A year later my posting is coming to an end and I am going back to head office in London. I am at my leaving dinner, hosted by the same CEO. We have continued to work together; the incident has never been mentioned.

Part 5: Walls in our hearts and minds…The Wall of Dis-Integrity

Though I would say he often seems a bit wary in my presence.

It is a big event, a sit down dinner in his home for at least 80 people. He gets to his feet towards the end of the meal and raises a hand to silence the live band. After a few of the usual clichés about my departure he turns to me.

"So Catherine, before you go, I have three questions for you. Why are you a vegetarian? Why are you a feminist? And can you really see auras?"

He sits down heavily as I start to stand. I am aware of cutlery clattering onto plates all around the room as people turn their attention to this promising situation. There are certainly people in the room who would get some pleasure from my humiliation.

So he has been saving it for this moment. Drawing attention to my three least acceptable, least corporate behaviours? Hoping for me to make a fool of myself?

My mind is racing. I have had to go from shock to fear, to trying to generate an answer in a matter of seconds. It feels like the whole room is holding its breath and I wish I had drunk less of his excellent wine. I doubt many of the people in the room are feminists. I know only one other is a vegetarian. As for the auras, who knows? When the culture doesn't allow that conversation it is hard to know how many people are secretly harbouring alternative views.

I aim for succinct and wry. I remember enough to avoid being defensive. The first two questions are easy enough to explain, I have been asked those before. As a woman in a male dominated industry in the 20th century it is a regular occurrence. And there have always been breakfast meetings, lunch meetings, dinner meetings. Too hard to hide being vegetarian. I take a chance on the last one.

"Yes I can read auras," I say, speaking directly to the CEO. "And so can you."

The room stirs and he stops mid sip of wine, the smug grin slipping a little. Clearly, he isn't expecting this answer. I quickly explain how understanding human nature is essential for every good salesperson or manager. Nobody can succeed in those fields without being able to read the energy of other people. "You might not know you can read auras," I observe with a smile, "but everybody else knows you can."

There was a minor repercussion when he tried to block my next promotion. But luckily I was able to

Part 5: Walls in our hearts and minds…The Wall of Dis-Integrity

outmanoeuvre that. And in the end, he only lasted another couple of years before his career with the company was ended.

I learnt an important lesson that day (apart from realising it might be best to keep my wits about me when I am at a leaving dinner where I might be asked to speak!). I realised that I can walk through that wall between my less conventional views and the rationality of the workplace. That the world is beginning to change, and it is becoming possible to integrate more of ourselves at work too.

It makes sense for us to bring our whole selves to our work, and it makes sense for the workplace to embrace and encourage that. I am reminded of the comment of a factory worker when we first started introducing a sustainability strategy to the business over twenty years ago. After listening carefully to the academic arguments and business rationale for sustainability he said, "So you mean instead of leaving our whole selves in the locker room when we get changed for the workday we act like actual human beings at work? Same as when we're at home?" So simple. So true.

Part 5: Walls in our hearts and minds…The Wall of Dis-Integrity

Wall of Dis-Integrity	
CAUSE: fear of expressing our full selves in front of others, especially at work or in societies where there is a strong prevailing "truth", the need to cover up inconvenient truths or living a double life	**COST:** not using all of an individual's talents and insights in any particular situation. Psychic cost and energy loss for the individual of living split lives.
Walking through the wall	
CODE: organisations communicating that all aspects of the person are acceptable. Even welcomed. Personal confidence / self-love, accepting ourselves exactly as we are	**BENEFITS:** more holistic solutions, more holistic employees, improved well-being, more effective use of resources

The Wall of Imposter Syndrome

Who among us has not experienced this one?

In a recent conversation with my closest friend (over 25
years together including family holidays, Christmas
dinners and the birth of my youngest) I was astonished to
hear her say

"I've never seen you express doubt. Never ever."

Yet from the inside I feel – like most of us - that I am in a
constant dialogue with that emotion (Am I enough? Am I
too much? Too young? Too old? Too naïve? Too jaded?
Talking too much? Being too quiet?... you know the
routine).

Yesterday an experienced life coach mentioned to me that
typically in his men's circles every single man, once he
feels safe, expresses how he thinks that the others all
know How to Be A Proper Man and only he is weak or
confused or struggling.

Not feeling good enough seems to be standard issue as
part of the human condition. In the shamanic tradition
even arrogance is seen as part of this aspect of our

Part 5: Walls in our hearts and minds…The Wall of Imposter Syndrome

humanity – a major cover-up job for the same feelings of self-doubt that the less confident may feel they display more obviously.

Is there anything we can do? Acknowledgement is a great first step. Then knowing that these are feelings not facts. I may *feel* that I don't deserve to be saying or doing or being this thing, but that is not the same as *not* deserving it. I may *feel* like an outsider, but that's not the same as having no value. Closely followed by remembering what a universal challenge this is.

If you knew for sure that this apparently confident and competent person in front of you in that meeting was definitely feeling imposter syndrome right now too, what might you do or say to them? How would that be different?

When we are feeling this way, most of our focus goes onto ourselves. And since the majority of our thoughts are negative (a leftover from the survival days of our early brain development, when being problem focused was literally a lifesaver) then the majority of our thoughts turned inward are also going to be negative. And we will be the focus of that negativity. So instead of the early stages of problem focus when our thoughts got us away from the poisonous snake or crumbling cliff edge, we now use a lot of that same urge on beating ourselves up. Listening to our inner critic. Accepting our own limiting beliefs.

Thankfully I notice this improves with age. So if you are in an earlier stage of your life, take heart. Keep doing the work and you will gradually feel better about yourself.

I notice that I went through stages with this. As a child I was so shy and unconfident that I struggled to say "present' when they called my name on the class register in school each morning. I was two thirds of the way through the list and spent the whole time preparing, dreading, practicing in my head. By the time it got to me my voice came out as a nervous squeak. "Catherine Shovlin?" enquired Sister Mary Veronica, directing the full force of her bushy eyebrows in my direction. "Yes" I whispered. She harumphed and carried on.

At the age of sixteen I got a job as a waitress. Partly to pay for eyeshadow and driving lessons. But also because I knew I would have to speak to strangers. I made myself do it. And I found that by adopting my cheerful waitress persona I could speak. Much later I heard Beyoncé being

interviewed on MTV (2006) and explaining her Sasha
Fierce persona.

"I'm really more quiet, reserved. I speak when spoken to
and polite. When I'm onstage, I'm aggressive, I'm strong,
I'm fearless. So I'm not who I really am in real life."

This was heartening news! If Beyoncé needs this kind of
self-talk to be the fabulous stage presence that she is, there
is hope for all of us.

The next stage of my emergence was going away to
university. I made a commitment to speaking to everyone
I stood next to for the first week. It was hard. Very hard. I
felt like the least cool person at the university. My clothes
were wrong. Turned out I knew nothing about the right
kind of music. And I never even knew I had an accent
from the north of England until everybody started
laughing at it. I definitely felt like an imposter. But I did it
anyway. And after a while, friends emerged from that
process. I couldn't wait till it felt ok to do that. I needed to
just start.

I joined some clubs and go along to a meeting of Amnesty
International. Most of what they are discussing is new to
me and I am shocked. How could anyone choose not to

do something? So much abuse of human rights in so many countries.

At the end of the meeting the chair turns to me.

"Well we are all in our final year now, so we really need to focus on studying and passing our exams. You seem to be on the right wavelength. Maybe you could take over the group Catherine?" (Yes, you're right, there is a pattern here!).

I protest of course. Most of what I know about human rights I have learned in the last two hours. And I have never run a group. Imposter Syndrome looms large and dark in my line of vision.

"You'll be fine," they assure me. "We'll be here if you need us. And of course we'll hand over all the materials."

I see now that what happened next is that my focus shifted from myself to the people we were trying to help. This wasn't about me, so I forgot about Imposter Syndrome. And over the next couple of years, as I struggled to drum up more membership (the posters I painstakingly created were often ripped down within a day by some of the more right wing groups on campus), connecting with HQ and organising speakers, going on

marches, attending AGMs and eventually ending up on
the national student committee, I didn't think much about
Imposter Syndrome at all. And what I did encounter were
many people who weren't that competent or amazing
after all. Union leaders, politicians, journalists… the
people I met at the national AGMs were remarkably
normal.

This then is another part of the code. Get to know people
at the top and you will probably be surprised at how
ungodlike they are. How they still make mistakes and
struggle to find the right words. Especially in real life,
without the benefit of an editing suite to repackage them
for the public. I say this not as a criticism of any of them –
we are all imposters, we are all doing our best, we are all
enough – but just to help calibrate.

It wasn't until I turned 50 that another shift happened.
Instead of being adept at acting like I felt alright and
behaving in a confident way, I suddenly actually *did* feel
alright. Something changed while I slept one night and
after all those years of faking it, I seem to have become
comfortable in my own skin. I realise now how the people
who always felt that find it so hard to relate to social
awkwardness and a sense of inadequacy. It's not about
being an introvert or an extrovert. It's about being you.

Part 5: Walls in our hearts and minds…The Wall of
Imposter Syndrome

You might want to try switching it up. First focus on
feeling kind towards the other person's imposter
syndrome (without telling them that's what you are doing
of course). Take a compassionate stance towards them
and feel how it shifts your own thoughts and feelings.
Then accept yourself with all your foibles and failings.
The more we learn to accept ourselves without judgment,
the easier it is to forget the habit of comparison and its
evil twin – finding things 'wrong' with the other person in
order to feel less bad about ourselves.

Sometimes trauma is part of the story too. So if that
applies to you, of course get the help you need to
complete your healing journey around that. I find EFT
(tapping) to be very useful. See my you tube channel
youtube.com/catherineshovlin for an introductory video,
or Udemy for my first aid level trauma release training
course https://www.udemy.com/course/trauma-
release/

At the end of the day we are all in the Game of Human
Life together. We are all imposters *and* we all belong. We
are all doing our best. Try approaching your own
imposter syndrome via someone else's and solve two
problems at once. Increase your empathy and feel more
comfortable in your own skin.

Part 5: Walls in our hearts and minds…The Wall of
Imposter Syndrome

Wall of Imposter Syndrome	
CAUSE: lack of self-esteem, criticism or lack of validation from parents, teachers, bosses, peers, social media, unconscious (and conscious) bias,	**COST:** outcasts, self-fulfilling failure, lack of self-actualisation, conformity, less free thinking in society, less creativity
Walking through the wall	
CODE: develop your own self to understand this inner glass ceiling and change it. Accept ourselves exactly as we are. Keep living, keep loving, shift is gradual but strong.	**BENEFITS:** more people achieve more, grow more, have more chance of self-fulfilment, better well being

The Wall of Shame

Oh yes. We all know this one. And thanks to Brené Brown's excellent body of work, we have all come to realise just how widespread this issue is. Our secret shame has become our acknowledged shame, and the wall gets less high with every realisation and acceptance of our own humanity.

My own experience is that shame puts a wall between me and the people I think are shaming me (they are usually not; it is mostly happening in my imagination). It can also generate lies - or at least half-truths and misrepresentation - which I then have to remember to be consistent about and plan around.

A couple of examples from my childhood.

"How often do you change your knickers?" asks one of my acquaintances, but not close friends, in the school playground. We are in Grade 6, so I am about 10 years old. She is addressing a small group of us. During the lunchtime break. We are not fans of tearing around playing chasey, so we tend to chat instead.

"Every day obviously!" retorts another friend immediately. What? Really? We always change our pants / underpants / briefs every second day and vests every third. Is that not normal? Is there something wrong with our family? Are we... God forbid…*Dirty?* The others concur with the daily change and all eyes turn on me.

"What about you Catherine?". I feel exposed, like they all already know the answer. Like the whole conversation is a set-up to humiliate and shame me. Don't go red, don't go red.

"Ha! Well, yeah. Every day. Obviously!!!". Too much? Too insincere? They all scrutinised me for a moment.

"Are you sure?" asks one.

"Yes of course. It would be yucky not to wouldn't it?"

Shame. I feel shame for wearing my knickers for two days. I feel shame on my mother for making me do that. And then more shame on myself for betraying my family. Shame on me for the look on my mother's face when I ask her later the same day why we wear our pants for two days.

The real shame of course is that I wasn't better equipped to deal with this situation. That I made it about me and my shortcomings instead of thinking it was a pretty intrusive question and not caring what answer I gave since it was none of their business.

Watching some of the Me-Too stories unfold in the last couple of years I notice some similarities (not in any way meaning to diminish the way women have been treated, just noticing some similar patterns). The sense of suddenly not knowing if what you always thought was ok and not ok was correct. The shifting sands. The uncertainty. The wish to fit in and the struggle to also be true to oneself. The feeling of not knowing the rules.

"If I say no will I get in trouble? Fired? Pushed off the project? But if I say yes will I lose credibility? Lose some part of my soul? I don't know which is the least bad option."

Given my general timidity in the first part of my life, I am relieved to look back at the 'nearly Me Too' situations I was in and wonder at how that version of myself had the courage to be so clear and protect herself. And I feel compassion and empathy for others who did not. The line is so thin and so hard to see. A slight concession becomes a slightly bigger concession and down the slippery slope we can go.

Another example that had repercussions for me is the incident of Tracy's Swings. Tracy was my best friend in the street. She was close to my age and had great toys and a relaxed home. Best of all, she had an excellent swing set in her back garden. My sister and I would often go round to her place to play and sometimes she would come to ours to have a go on our climbing frame.

We see their car (an enviably stylish purple Ford Cortina) go past our house and know they have gone out for the day. The temptation is excruciating. Eventually we cave and saunter casually up the road then sneak down the side alley into their back garden. Oh the glory of those swings all to ourselves. No waiting for a turn. Free flight. Jumping off without worrying about landing badly and looking silly. We have a glorious time.

Until we hear the car pull into the driveway. We freeze. There is no way out except to walk right past them. They will see us as soon as they walk into the modern open plan house. Like rabbits in the headlights we just stare at each other in horror as Tracy's mother comes round the corner and sees us. Of course she reads us the riot act and we snivel and grovel then scarper.

Now I am a parent and adult myself, I know how common this situation is. Kids push boundaries and adults push back. It's not such a big deal. It's how they learn what is ok and what is not.

But at this time, my sister and I are mortified. We hide in the utility room for hours. Crouched down in the corner behind the spin dryer, where we can't be seen. Waiting to hear if she will come round to tell our parents what terrible children we are. Waiting for punishment to fall from the sky.

I look at my watch.

"It's been three hours, maybe we should go in the house? We can't stay here for ever."

Nervously we tiptoe into the kitchen. My parents are surprised and a little worried that we've been gone so long. But playing out most of the day is completely normal in the 1970s. We are subdued and worried. We whisper about it in our bunk beds at night. I remember at some point much later saying "Well it's been two years now… maybe it's ok? Maybe she has forgiven us?"

When we move to a new house a few years later we feel we can make a fresh start.

Part 5: Walls in our hearts and minds…The Wall of Shame

One of the walls that were built that day were between me and my friend Tracy – our friendship was never the same once I was obsessed with avoiding her mother! Another was between me and my sister and our parents. We felt we had let them down so badly that we stepped away a little. Hiding behind the Wall of Shame. Keeping secrets.

Now I cannot believe the enormity of our response. The mismatch with the crime. The amount of emotional energy we wasted on an event which most likely barely made a mark on the other family's lives. It is, frankly, ridiculous. But I won't make shame out of my shame. We can too easily recycle that and get into a shame cycle that might go on for ever. I can only turn to that younger self and offer her love and compassion and remind her that she is enough, that she is ok. I can only learn from this and all the other childhood incidents when shame weighed most heavily on my shoulders.

I'm sure you have your own stories too. Maybe some seem silly, like these, when you look back at them as your grown self. Others may be enormous, possibly overwhelming if you haven't processed the trauma around them. It may be worth finding support to do that if you want to walk through this wall.

It is a worthwhile exercise to visit that younger version as the older, wiser person you now are. What would you say to that child filled with shame? Encourage them to share how they feel. Embrace them with love and acceptance. Remind them of all the wonderful things they are and will become. Maybe this incident is a clue to a future strength in their character. Love them. Accept them. Understand how they feel and ask them what they need. Promise to be by their side.

It is my experience that this kind of revisiting has an extraordinary power to heal. A kind of Butterfly Effect where, by changing one emotional reaction in our past, we reprogram a whole bunch of things that happened to us since then and end up in a slightly different place in the multiverse.

You might not buy into that view, but I believe you will still find comfort in this process.

Wall of Shame	
CAUSE: low self-esteem, lack of information, sensitivity, dwelling on mistakes, blaming ourselves for things that are not our fault	**COST:** shrinking back, reduction in capability, risk avoidance, resistance to situations
Walking through the wall	
CODE: self-love, accepting ourselves exactly as we are, revisiting the self in that moment and comforting / accepting / understanding them	**BENEFITS:** the ability to learn, move on and thrive, judge ourselves less so others less, shame ourselves less so others less

The Wall of Scarcity

Oh this one kept me hemmed in for a long time. It served some purpose – it gave me drive, it made me work harder, spend less, invest more and build a position where now I have a lot more options. All to the good.

But the Wall of Scarcity is put up around us by consumerism and the media. Look how happy this guy is with his new car. Look how much better these people are dressed. Look how much fun everyone is having on social media. Look at how successful this woman is despite having lost her leg as a child. Look at this perfect family. We all get exposed repeatedly to the triple whammy of scarcity:

> You don't *have* enough.

> You don't *do* enough.

> *You* are not enough.

We soak it up every day. Each time we switch on the TV or check out our social media or walk past a shop. When we say "I want…" we may not realise the exact meaning of the word. We are identifying ourselves as wanting.

Part 5: Walls in our hearts and minds…The Wall of Scarcity

Missing something. Not being enough. Just look at the dictionary definition:

want ing

1. **absent; lacking; missing**: a coat with some buttons WANTING
2. **not up to some standard; inadequate** in some essential: weighed and found WANTING
3. **lacking** (something); without: a watch WANTING a minute hand
4. **minus; less**: a year WANTING two weeks

None of these are states any of us would enjoy being in or being seen as.

The origin of the word desire on the other hand is from the Latin meaning *"await what the stars will bring"* – definitely a more enticing concept. So one way we can walk through the wall of scarcity is to start talking about our desires rather than our wants.

It struck me the other day how absurd the catchphrase "because you're worth it" is. I'm worth a $10 pot of cream? Heck no. I'm worth way more than that. So are you. So is anybody and everybody. But our limbic brain responds – maybe this will make me beautiful / happy /

Part 5: Walls in our hearts and minds…The Wall of Scarcity

loved. Is it worth another hour working a job you hate? Is it worth more than investing in renewable energy? More than saving up to travel or learn or hang out with your friends?

Walking through the Wall of Scarcity to the land of abundance takes awareness and courage. My head went through the wall a long time ago, I got the idea, I *understood* it. But it has taken me much longer to get my heart, my guts, my soul through that wall. Life is so much sweeter once the wall is gone.

Two events that helped me find my way.

A couple of years ago, I hired Sarah Bickers, a de-cluttering expert to help me reduce the amount of unnecessary things in my house. Large house, 3 kids, many hobbies plus scarcity mindset equals an awful lot of stuff. Not quite hoarding. But in that direction. Aided and abetted by the voices in my head

"Waste not want not",

"You never know when that will come in handy",

"Remember the sugar shortage?"

Part 5: Walls in our hearts and minds…The Wall of Scarcity

For those who weren't living through that last example, it caused a lot of panic buying and had a major impact on jam making activities in the UK in 1974. The toilet roll fiasco of 2020 is similar evidence.

So while you could walk into my house and ask if you could have that picture, that scarf, that packet of flour, and I'd pretty much always say yes, while I am happy to cart sackfuls of clothes to the charity (goodwill) shop, I can't bring myself to send things to landfill. To just declare them utterly useless.

Luckily for me Sarah (freeyourspace.co.uk) is an expert in this kind of thing. She has already heard every excuse I can come up with and has strategies for all of them. We get rid of 92 sacks of stuff in the end, and only 5 of those go to landfill. Not bad. It helps that I live in a neighbourhood where almost anything I put on my front wall is of interest to someone and disappears within a few hours.

Among that process, we come across a notebook. A beautiful notebook. She picks it up and flicks through. It is completely unused.

Part 5: Walls in our hearts and minds…The Wall of Scarcity

"What about this? Shall I put it in your office for making notes? Or throw it in the recycling bag?" she asks, completely reasonably.

"I'm saving it" I replied.

"For what?"

"For a special occasion. It's too nice to use"

"I see. Do you remember when you bought it?"

"Yes! On holiday….er… in 1979"

She doesn't really need to say anything else. She just gives me the look. Umm. There is the problem clear as day. My wall of scarcity looms over me. I would have found it easier to put a valuable piece of jewellery on my front wall for a passer-by to take than to do the same with this notebook.

I think back to 1979. The whole country was in scarcity mindset. Industries like mining, shipbuilding and steel making were all closing or in dire straits. There was creativity in music (punk and new romantics) and alternative comedy for sure, but the general state was of pessimism and fear. We had suffered recessions in the UK 1973-75 and were heading to the 1980 one. My family was

Part 5: Walls in our hearts and minds…The Wall of Scarcity

ok, but we weren't flush with money. My parents were good stewards of their funds and managed well by being aware of spending. So the water I was swimming in was not flavoured with abundance.

Since then we have had a couple more recessions and are now well into the 2020 COVID-19 one. How has the pandemic affected you? More scarcity (focusing on the constraints and limitations) or more abundance (thinking of all the new time that has opened up for family, home, nature, reflection, the realisation that you don't need to spend money and get more stuff in order to be happy – or sad)?

Whatever the social and financial position of people I know, I notice an emphasising effect of COVID on their existing personality traits. The happy, positive outlook people I know have loved the pause, the break from the rat race, the rediscovering of simple pleasures in life. While others focusing on what is not possible and feeding the fear via the endless, confusing news cycle, have found it much harder.

Meanwhile, back in 2018…the notebook is beautiful. Which means it cost me maybe as much as five ordinary ones that would have done the same job without the

Part 5: Walls in our hearts and minds…The Wall of Scarcity

aesthetic value. It was extremely precious to me at the time of purchase, and now, nearly 40 years later, it has benefitted from scarcity inflation and feels just as significant as it did when I bought it. Coming face to face with the scarcity wall is a turning point for me.

From that moment, I start using the things I have. Wearing my "just for best" clothes. Enjoying that fancy face cream I've been given. I set an intention of using everything I have. If I wear that normally-expensive-but-reduced-in-the-sale cardigan that I have never used and enjoy it, that is great. If I don't then it can go to a friend who it is perfect for, or the charity shop. I start whittling down what I have. And overcoming the urge to stockpile.

As Sarah kindly points out, I do live in London - a world city. In 15 minutes I can be in any one of a very large number of shops. I have credit cards and transport. If I really need something – pretty much anything - I can get it very easily. There is no need to hold on to so much "*just in case*".

When she says all that to me my brain agrees with her – it is logical, it makes sense. But something else is clinging. I still feel a lot of attachment to the stuff that is still in the house. The direction of travel has been halted though; I

Part 5: Walls in our hearts and minds…The Wall of Scarcity

am slowly making a turn around. After her visit I discipline myself to clear out another bagful each week – but I do it like a reluctant exerciser might drag themselves to the gym because they know they should.

And now, I am writing this in Bali. I came just before the start of COVID-19 and then circumstances have conspired to keep me here for many months. I was just coming on holiday, so I had a 22kg (50lb) bag. If I had known how long I would end up staying, I would have spent a lot more time deciding what to bring. I probably would have brought more than the one pair of flipflops that I have worn every day for months now. But beyond that I haven't really missed anything.

In fact, the opposite has been true. It has been a pleasure living from one small cupboard of clothes instead of drawers and drawers of choice. I use a fraction of the headspace on deciding what to wear since the options are limited. It helps of course that it is a tropical climate and I am dressing in casual clothes, not workwear. But even so, picking one t-shirt from four options is a lot easier than one from 10 or 20.

Check out the maths. If each top goes with each skirt / shorts / trousers (unlikely but bear with me) and I have 5 tops and 5 bottoms, that is 25 possible combinations to pick from. Even just doubling that to 10 tops and 10 bottoms knocks the number of combinations up to 100 – 4 times the brain effort to decide.

If I am completely honest about my usual wardrobe and include things I hardly ever wear, it is probably more like 50 by 50 – that is 2500 possible combinations. So my dressing decision each morning is 100 times less complicated here in Bali than in my 'usual' life.

Add to that the fact of 2 identical coffee mugs instead of dozens, one pair of flipflops instead of 30 pairs of shoes, 2 bags instead of 20… and I realise what a very big clear out I will be having when I get back to the UK one day.

Bali has helped me shift my entire perspective to abundance. It's a feeling not a fact. Now, I get it. Now I feel abundance not scarcity inside me and I can shed things with grace and humour. Gifting them to someone who needs them more. Being abundant, sharing abundance, living and breathing abundance. It is a massive improvement.

The other wall of scarcity I have learned to walk through is around financial abundance.

Part 5: Walls in our hearts and minds…The Wall of Scarcity

Nearly twenty years ago I came into a significant amount of money. More than I had ever had or earned. I was still entrenched in scarcity mindset at that time and immediately associated the money with negative feelings. I felt beholden, that it was a transaction that I would need to repay. I felt offended, that it implied I couldn't manage on my own. I felt unworthy of the gift.

I felt it made me into a bad person (*money is the root of all evil, it is easier for a camel to pass through the eye of a needle than for a rich man to enter heaven, you can't be rich and good etc…* I italicise because I now know these are misinterpretations). Nobody I knew had this kind of money in their bank account. It felt like hot potatoes, ill-gotten gains, though it was nothing of the sort.

Basically I couldn't incorporate it into my self-view. It crashed headlong into my limiting beliefs (see next chapter) and made me feel very uncomfortable.

So I decided to invest the money. Not, as I had with my own money, into UK property that I redeveloped successfully on my own, but into Other People's Schemes.

I knew better than to put all my eggs in one basket so over the next 12 months I read a lot, attended a lot of presentations and selected ten different projects spanning three continents. Definitely a spread. I did my analysis, risk assessment, I did the sums and the due diligence

All but one of those investments was a failure. Several turned out to be scams and others were just bad ideas. One house was swept away by the 2004 tsunami. There are still three ongoing court cases. If I had tried to "lose" that much money I would have been hard pressed to know how to do so. It would have been better to just give it all to charity. I did gift a chunk of it… but I thought I was investing for my family's future security.

I now realise that the reason for this poor result was not bad judgement (my other investment decisions have had a 90% success rate) or bad luck. It was my attitude to abundance. My own resistance to financial abundance, and all the blockages and limiting beliefs that stood between me and acceptance.

Last year I decided I could have money. That it did not make me a bad person. Having money gives me the freedom to do voluntary work, to help communities develop projects and to share my knowledge regardless of someone's ability to pay. As part of that shift I decided I could, against the odds, recover some of the money now. That it was still in the universe with some connection to me. Some of it is a lost cause, but I got or am likely to get compensation money for some of the ten. This time I will receive it with grace and a positive attitude! This time I will be thankful and appreciate the opportunities it gives me. I will use it as a chance to practise abundance thinking.

We all have our own take on scarcity. Do you feel there's no jobs for you? That all the good men (or women) are taken? That there's never enough time in the day? I invite you to consider how it would be to walk through that wall. To treasure the love you do have in your life. The hours of each day. All the people you are connected with. Or try Deepak Chopra's 21 day Abundance Challenge. It worked for me, maybe it will for you too.

Part 5: Walls in our hearts and minds…The Wall of Scarcity

Wall of Scarcity	
CAUSE: times of hardship, inherited attitude of hardship, media and advertising, unrealistic models of looks / happiness / attainment on social media	**COST:** sense of inadequacy, state of being in want, always striving, never contented, eating disorders, rivalry, jealousy, getting into unnecessary debt
Walking through the wall	
CODE: self-love, accepting ourselves exactly as we are, believing we *are* enough, we *do* enough, we *have* enough	**BENEFITS:** the ability to enjoy what we have with gratitude and grace, a more positive attitude to life and each other, less stress

The Wall of Limiting Beliefs

The process of shaking off limiting beliefs is like walking
up a round topped hill. You think you can see the summit
but when you walk on a bit further you realise there is
more. And then more. It is an ongoing journey which can
seem overwhelming. But bear in mind that at every stage
you are further forward than before. The continuing
nature of the quest does not make it any less worthwhile
and there are benefits every step of the way.

The big challenge for me has been getting any of my
limiting beliefs cleared, not from my brain – there is
usually a pretty clear case for why they should go which
my thought processes have no problem agreeing with –
but from my body.

We store so much emotion and so many beliefs in our
physical body – often without realising it. Insults that we
pretended didn't affect us at the time, moments of shame,
a sense of being judged, admonishments, disappointment,
being hurt by people. And all the rest. While we may
rationalise the experience with bravado or justifications:

Part 5: Walls in our hearts and minds…The Wall of Limiting Beliefs

"What do I care if he thinks I'm not a tough manager? He's an idiot anyway"

We may still have swallowed it. Almost literally. It has become part of us. Messages we received as a baby and child that we may not even remember, are still part of the fabric of our being. If your belief system allows the possibility of past lives, then there are also those memories and experiences to consider.

I strongly believe that all bodies should have the same access to education, jobs, financial empowerment, voting and whatever else in the world may have been at one time the domain of powerful white able-bodied men. I have fought for change in the workplace and try to live by this belief.

Yet in a recent healing I discovered things about the dominance of my right (masculine) side of my body over my left (feminine) side of my body that shocked me. I realised I had absorbed those messages from society about male and female. Even though that wasn't in play in my home or school. And the righthand side of my body really thought it had to take care of everything while the left-hand side felt weak.

Part 5: Walls in our hearts and minds…The Wall of Limiting Beliefs

The Thesaurus website has been changed now but this definition still lurks in their link in google searches, testimony to how recently views have shifted:

Synonyms for **powerless** at Thesaurus.com … *adj.weak; unable … With all his powers of intellect, he was powerless, because he had no faith in virtue. … drained · effeminate · effete · emasculate · enervated · exhausted · faint · feeble · feminine · flaccid · frail · powerless …*

Too many of those words offered as alternatives for 'powerless' are to do with feminine energy, or a lack of masculine energy.

So billions of us have grown up with these labels. Similar situations exist in relation to being black, disabled, mentally ill, of a particular religion of nationality or racial group, a spinster, too short, too tall, too intelligent, not academic, not sporty… so many more categories that come with their own special package of allegedly correlated characteristics.

As our evolution continues to progress, and especially in the last 100 years, many of these views have been called to account. But remnants remain in books, in people's minds, in legislation, in the media and therefore in attitudes. It is a big job to change all of that (a worthwhile

challenge of course) but meanwhile we can start with
ourselves.

Addressing our own limiting beliefs about what we are
allowed or capable of doing, and we are taking steps
towards releasing them in society too.

I find it helps to focus on an arising issue. A situation I am
experiencing where I feel – even momentarily - that I
cannot do something. Pause. What is happening? What
limiting belief does this evidence? Is it valid? Is it
relevant? Does it matter? Does it merit being the arbiter of
this decision? Often not.

For example there is the fact that I have been in Bali
during COVID-19. Where restrictions are minimal,
healing is everywhere, food is natural and healthful,
people are nearly always compassionate and calm – and
the cafes stayed open. I am acutely aware that life has not
been so sweet everywhere in the world. Especially for
those contracting the disease or caring for the sick. Or
losing their job or business from the effects of lockdown. I
know there has been a lot of suffering.

So part of me thinks I should be suffering too. That it is
unfair that I should be ok while others are not. My brain
knows that this doesn't make a lot of sense, that it doesn't

Part 5: Walls in our hearts and minds...The Wall of Limiting Beliefs

help anyone else if I also suffer. And of course, I have helped others where I can, in the countries I am most closely connected with. My conscience is clear.

But when the airport reopened and the possibility of flying back to London became a reality, I struggled with my desire to stay. Eventually I recognised that my primary motivation to leave was guilt – garnished with a limiting belief that I can't have it this good. All those phrases in our subconscious - *too good to be true, alright for some, looking after #1* and the rest - echoed in my head and created a wall between me and my desire. Between what I thought I should do and what I wanted to do.

At some level, I did not *believe* that I was allowed to do what I wanted. Even though it wasn't harming anybody and I was making a contribution to the struggling Balinese economy. Even though my spiritual view is of connection and unity so each individual can contribute to the total sum of happiness of the human race by increasing their own (so long as that isn't at anyone's expense).

The wall of limiting beliefs was looming over me and making it hard to see the way forward.

Part 5: Walls in our hearts and minds…The Wall of Limiting Beliefs

I am still here, so you know that I managed to walk through that particular wall. I have even stopped apologising for my good fortune.

There are many of these walls based on our many limiting beliefs. They lie in wait, ready to spring up at a moment's notice to block our path. It is a lifelong project to spot them and walk through them. And that is ok. While we are alive, we can always grow and learn. Every wall you walk through makes you stronger.

Part 5: Walls in our hearts and minds…The Wall of Limiting Beliefs

Wall of Limiting Beliefs	
CAUSE: programming in childhood, bullying, abuse, school, racism, sexism, religious beliefs and all other social biases	**COST:** misery, waste of human potential, passing on of beliefs to next generation, blame, resentment, victim mentality
Walking through the wall	
CODE: identifying and challenging our limiting beliefs one by one, time after time. Without judging ourselves for having held them.	**BENEFITS:** the ability to thrive and be our best selves – for our own sake and for the good of society

The Wall of Perfection

A commonly used concept in advertising these days, especially of female beauty products, is perfection. A flawless complexion. Immaculate eyebrows. A perfect tan.

Nature is not perfect. Humans are not perfect. In fact who would want to meet a perfect human (in the unlikely event that we could agree on what that was)? They would be creepy and terrifying.

And yet so many of us feel that we are the only one not achieving the required standard. There is a wall separating us (the inadequate) from them (the perfect). We all feel on the wrong side of the wall, at least some of the time, with our mismatched clothes and wonky nose and secret KitKat habit. While over there, on the other side, the Perfect People are getting everything right. As a society, we have been pretty much trained to think this way since birth.

I do see different versions of it around the world. White people using fake tan to be perfect, darker skinned people using lightening creams to be perfect, straight haired people curling their hair while curly haired people straighten it. The Berbers see brown teeth as a form of beauty, the Victorians valued black teeth as it meant you could afford the luxury of sugar… and we whiten our teeth. When I was growing up, we aspired towards slim eyebrows and a small bottom. Now my daughters want the opposite.

Clearly 'perfect' is not a fixed idea.

There are signs of a few bricks in this wall being dislodged. Recent comedy and drama series show imperfect people making mistakes and feeling lousy. According to Judd Apatow, co-creator of TV shows like Girls, and Love, one of the reasons we laugh at comedy is the recognition of the emotion and the realisation that "It's not just me?!" It is such a relief to find out we are not the only person in the world who has these feelings, these near misses, these moments of complete unknowing, that we burst out laughing. And since laughter stimulates the immune system, improves respiration and exercises our abs, that's a pretty good result.

A short cut to walking through this particular wall might be just to laugh more. I have been trying this out…

I am on my way to pitch to the Department of Education. This has required 3 trains and a taxi ride. My outfit is

Part 5: Walls in our hearts and minds…The Wall of Perfection

perfect. My hair is – for once - cooperating. I feel a little nervous, but I know I have checked my presentation thoroughly for spelling mistakes and incoherence. Everything is perfect. So why do I not feel completely present? I walk up the steps of their entrance, feeling a little disembodied, a little numb.

As I step through the portal into the vast entry foyer, scanning for the security desk I feel a slipping sensation. My knickers (briefs, underpants) have chosen this exact moment to abandon the idea of elasticity and drop to my ankles! Definitely not perfection.

With a broad smile (well I feel like I've slipped into a Bridget Jones movie, I have to laugh) I click my high heels and step out of the offending underwear before flicking it swiftly into my briefcase.

It was the kind of moment that seems like a disaster. But actually it brought me to a very different state. Alert, responsive, fired up and ready to go. Nobody but me (and a few dozen people who were in the entry foyer at the time but not, thankfully, attending my presentation) knew that I was going commando during my pitch. And I smoothly managed to whisk the handouts from my briefcase without also serving up my knickers. And yes, I got the business. With enough profit margin to update my underwear drawer!

Kicking the wall of perfection out of your way will give you a happier, healthier and quite possibly more successful life. Good enough is good enough whether that is your parenting, your gardening, your thesis or that very special home-cooked dinner.

Enjoy all that is right or smart or beautiful in the moment. *And* all that is wrong or dumb or messy too. Celebrate all of it and laugh out loud in the face of challenges.

Part 5: Walls in our hearts and minds…The Wall of Perfection

Wall of Perfection	
CAUSE: unrealistic imagery and portrayals in media and social media, lack of self-esteem, criticism in early years	**COST:** anxiety, reduction in well-being, overspend on 'solutions', critical of self and therefore of others, lower immunity
Walking through the wall	
CODE: self-love, accepting ourselves exactly as we are, accepting that humans are meant to be perfectly imperfect. Ourselves first and then others.	**BENEFITS:** improved well-being, the ability to thrive, more compassion for others, less urge for comparison and outdoing or doing down

Part 6:
Now walk through walls…The Wall of Perfection

Part 6: Now Walk through Walls

...

Developing the art

As you have seen, walking through walls has a great deal to recommend it. Maybe it seems like a no-brainer. And yet, both within ourselves and within our societies and their organisations, there is resistance.

It is true that there is something comforting about walls. The home and style magazines sometimes refer to *hygge* and in that sense, walls can invoke a sense of protection, safety and predictability.

> Hygge (/ˈh(j)uːgə/; Danish: [ˈhykə]; Norwegian: [ˈhŷɡːə]) is a Danish and Norwegian word for a mood of cosiness and comfortable conviviality with feelings of wellness and contentment.

We all need a balance between a safe foundation and bold exploration. Too much of the former might make us so comfortable we get complacent and allow our transformative power and appetite for self-actualisation to atrophy. Too much of the latter can leave us vulnerable and unstable. I like the *feng shui* concept (if not the language) of the "commanding position". One where you have a wall behind you to lean on and openness in front

Part 6:
Now walk through walls...Developing the art

of you. You may notice that you feel more comfortable on a couch with its back to the wall than one with the door behind it.

In a similar vein, Zen master Joan Halifax, an inspirational source of wisdom during my End of Life Doula (death companion) training, uses the term *"soft front, strong back"*. As she explains,

> "Soft front, strong back is about the relationship between equanimity and compassion. 'Strong back' is equanimity and your capacity to really uphold yourself. 'Soft front' is opening to things as they are."

In Zen Yoga, there is a corresponding concept relating to the energy body and its circulation system.

- *Toko myaku* channel, runs down the back of the body, and protects us. It is tough, masculine, yang energy.
- *Nin myaku:* channel runs down the front of the body. This is reflected in everyday sayings like *"baring one's chest"*. It has a more feminine, open, connecting yin energy.

There are benefits to having foundations, some protection, some stability, a wall that has "got your back". And often

Part 6:
Now walk through walls…Developing the art

it is good to have an open view in front. No restrictions.
No hidden surprises.

Walls have benefits as well as hazards. Next time you
become aware of a wall – which I hope you are more
likely to do now – then all I suggest is that you consider it.

Is this a wall that is protecting you? And if so, is it
protection from a genuine threat (like a sea wall to stop
the high tides washing away the town) or is it a shielding
wall that maybe used to have a real purpose which is now
no longer the case? Or was generated by others as a way
of constraining or controlling you? Governments
sometimes speak of building actual walls around
countries, but more often they create protectionist walls
by subsidising domestic production, placing punitive
taxes on imported products or introducing strict and
complex entry requirements.

During the 2020 pandemic these walls came clanging into
play all over the world as nationals were encouraged to
repatriate and foreigners blocked from entering other
countries. The free-flow of people and goods that we have
enjoyed for years now, came to a sudden halt. Poor
countries with a dependency on foreign spending from
tourists were left high and dry.

Part 6:
Now walk through walls…Developing the art

There are certainly issues with globalisation, but now we have seen what happens when it stops. When money stops circulating the economy declines. Not to say that economic growth is always a good idea, but the change requires adjustment and it looks like being a slow process for policies and attitudes to catch up and evolve.

But back to you and me. Next time you notice a physical, political or social wall, try asking yourself - is this a wall I want to keep in my life? Or one which I might try walking through? How might the removal of that wall help both the people on your side and those beyond the wall? What stuck ideas and attitudes are we perpetrating each time we just accept a wall without challenge?

There are many walls that you might not be able to do much about. At least in the short term. But the more of us who see them, the more we can be aware of their effect on us. And the sum of many voices is a loud noise. Enough to break down a wall.

Some walls are necessary. Privacy or safety or warmth are sometimes exactly what is needed. Others have outlived their usefulness and are just there because they always were. As we humans continue our never-ending journey of evolution, I invite you to check out the walls you see

Part 6:
Now walk through walls…Developing the art

around you and see which ones you, and others, might benefit from you walking through.

If you walk through a wall, do it in a way that you can take others with you. Break down barriers and division and consider each other's point of view. Let the light shine through. It's a liberating feeling!

Any Wall	
CAUSE: misunderstandings, poor information, fear, low self-esteem	**COST:** reduction in capacity for the individual and for the human race.
Walking through the wall	
CODE: love of self and of others	**BENEFITS:** thriving together

Part 6:
Now walk through walls…Epilogue: The Wall of War

Epilogue: The Wall of War

Kahina makes her way back from the market with a heavy basket of vegetables, the fingers of her free hand trailing along the dusty stone of The Wall. She hums softly to herself and doesn't notice her aunt approaching until she feels the bony finger jab her in the arm.

"Dreaming again Kahina? What are you like! Your poor mother and father. I don't know what they did to deserve you!" she waddles off cackling loudly at her succinct character assassination.

Blowing her hair out of her eyes, the intended insult sliding straight off her, the young woman continues her way home, dropping the bag of market produce onto the dirt floor of their kitchen area with a thud.

Her mother is bustling around as usual, chattering about the neighbours, the heat – were the rains ever coming? – the naughtiness of Kahina's baby brother. She barely registers most of it as she sits on the floor slicing carrots for their soup that evening.

"And Those People!" exclaims her mother, with a knowing swing of her eyes to the west. "They're getting louder and louder. It's ridiculous. You'll see! It's getting dark already and they start up that hullaballoo. Drums and wailing and goddess knows what. I ask you. Where's it all going to end? It didn't used to be like this."

Kahina smiles to herself. She has lived her whole life in this town. Nestled between The Wall and the beginnings of the desert mountains. Nobody even knows when the wall was built, far less why. It has always been there, snaking off into the distance to the north and the south. Too high to see over, even with the tallest ladder. And the boys have tried their best, tottering piles of them on each other's shoulders. They don't even come close.

Nobody has ever seen the Other Side, but they know that Those People live there. They hear them, clanging about. They hear their donkeys braying and their kids shouting. Most of all they hear their ceremonies every night just after dark falls with the abrupt suddenness of the desert.

She has always just accepted this set up. Like all the people in their town it seems normal. It has always been like that. But she senses some shift in attitudes these days.

"Bloody hell!" the curse announces the arrival of her father, back from the fields. "The water's down again!" he announces. "We've wasted nearly the whole day deepening the well. It's nearly twice as deep now as it was when I was a lad. Those People are to blame. I'm sure of it."

Her mother clucks and fusses around him. Bringing water to wash his blistered feet and hands, making soothing noises as he continues his diatribe. "I'm not kidding Rosa," he says at one point. "Something has to be done. Things can't carry on like this."

Like what? Wonders Kahina as she stirs the soup. Aksil tears through the cooking area, a long stick held high above his head and a warrior's roar on his three-year old face. "Let's fight them Dada! Let's get our water back!"

The next day, she and her family have their usual early start. Feeling her way through the narrow alleys in the dark, Aksil pulling on her hand, too slow as always. "Come on" she urges him, wishing her father hadn't said she couldn't just carry him like before. Apparently, it is high time he learnt to be a man and walked on his own two feet. "Hurry up! You know we have to be there to make the sun rise."

Later, when all her chores are done and she is on her way back from calligraphy lessons, Kahina stops in her favourite spot. The olive trees shield her from the

Part 6:
Now walk through walls…Epilogue: The Wall of War

townsfolk and she leans back against The Wall, sun warmed by this time in the early afternoon.

She places the flat of her hand against its rough-hewn stone. Sensing what could be on the side. What Those People might be like. Rumour had it they were deformed, twisted versions of people. Not quite right. Prone to drinking their home brewed spirits and talking to ghosts. She shudders slightly at the thought.

What can you see, hand? She muses. But the hand just sees ordinary people living ordinary lives. That can't be right. Can it? What about all the stories? The terrible events from the other side of The Wall that her town talks about regularly.

Izil stirs in his sleep. It's not even light yet but they've started already. He groans and rolls over on his straw pallet. It's infuriating. Why don't they just wait till morning to do whatever strange things they do on the other side of This Wall. But no, there they go The Others with their pipes and drums and whoever is in charge of that endless high-pitched singing. Grr.

Maybe his older brother is right, he considers. Maybe it is about time they broke through This Wall at the Eastern edge of their town and gave The Others a good seeing to.

Part 6:
Now walk through walls…Epilogue: The Wall of War

They could get all their stuff and make slaves of them said his brother, laughing heartily at the thought.

Could they really be that bad? wonders Izil. He has lived in this town all his life, between This Wall to the east and the high hills before the coast to the west. He has tried many times to scale This Wall. He and his friends even tried making a kind of catapult once, to launch themselves onto the top of it. That hadn't ended well.

He decides he may as well get up. There are the goats to see to and his shift on wolf watch later. It is hours until he gets to sit down again. The sun is past its peak but still strong. No shade now until dark but there's a patch by the water hole that isn't quite as hot. He leans his back against This Wall and tries to imagine what is on the other side. His uncle is the town scholar and has written lengthy descriptions of the strange bewitched people on the other side of the wall. Babies born that would fit in your hand. Old women with long greenish hair reaching all the way to the ground. Is that true? He has never known anything different but somehow it just doesn't sit right with him. He turns a little and presses the flat of his hand against This Wall. Trying to see. Then realises sunset is not far off and he needs to get to the town square for the daily ceremony urging it to return the next day.

Part 6:
Now walk through walls…Epilogue: The Wall of War

Something pulls him back to this spot. Day after day. It's almost like he can feel something in This Wall. He presses his palm against it again. Yes, there's something. Some kind of energy.

"Hello?" he says quietly. Tentatively.

"Hello," comes the reply.

On their respective sides of the wall, Kahina and Izil pull back in shock. Then lean against it again.

"Are you there?"

"I am here"

Over the following days and weeks they meet every afternoon. She on her side of the wall in the east town and he on his in the west. They feel so much energy between their hands that it is like the wall is dissolving between them. They speak of the goats and the insects and the rains that are now hovering in the distance. They both long for their meetings, rushing through their chores and throwing vague excuses at their families as they hurry to the spot where the olive trees grow by the water hole. On the east and on the west.

"I have to see you," he whispers to This Wall.

Part 6:
Now walk through walls...Epilogue: The Wall of War

"I long to hold your hand," she replies to The Wall.

She forgets that he is one of Those People and he forgets that she is one of The Others.

Meanwhile their friends and families prepare for battle. The air is tense with hope and fear. Rumours are circulating on the western side of That Wall, suggesting large number so people are dying from are mysterious disease coming from The Others. Izil doesn't actually know anybody who has died but everybody is talking about it. Apparently, The Others have poisoned the water supply. They have to be stopped. War is the only way, according to his brother. "They're not even like real people anyway," he said at breakfast this morning. "You know, they're weird. Not really human. We need to fix them once and for all."

"What are we to do?" she wonders, leaning against The Wall, her eyes focusing in the middle distance. Just that morning her aunt had assailed her in the market with a story about goat flu.

"It's Those People" she had muttered darkly, jabbing Kahina's arm for emphasis. "At night, after they make all that racket, they throw poisoned meat over the wall and our goats eat it and then they get sick and then they make

Part 6:
Now walk through walls…Epilogue: The Wall of War

us sick and we are all going to die. All going to die I tell you! They must be stopped."

"Who has died Auntie?" Kahina asks. The older woman rolls her eyes in disdain. "Lots of people," she assures her niece. "The butcher's cousin's neighbour died. And that woman who lives down by the river with all the children. Some of them I think…" She peters out, trying to get her facts straight.

Placing her hand flat against The Wall she feels the energy. She knows he is there. She yearns to see him. Suddenly she has an idea. So obvious she can't imagine why it didn't occur to her before.

"The hills!" she whispers urgently at the wall as she scrambles to her feet. Hearing movement on the other side she hopes he has heard.

It takes her most of the afternoon to climb up the beginnings of the mountains. Along goat tracks, past scrubby bushes until even they give up. Her leather sandals are of little use on the rough stones, but she continues. Up and up and up.

Eventually she can go no further. She turns in the late afternoon sun as thunder claps on the horizon and a

Part 6:
Now walk through walls…Epilogue: The Wall of War

rainstorm threatens to start further down the valley. The sun warms the earth and she sees that there are, just as she had hoped, mountains on the other side of The Wall too. She can't see the town or Those People, the wall is too high, even from here. But she can see the hills beyond.

It is so far. How will they see each other. Then her eyes are snagged by a flash of yellow. A ripple of cloth blowing out across the top of the hill. A makeshift flag marking his presence. "Yes!". What can she do? Realising how horrified her father would be she yanks off her red winding cloth under her skirts. It is longer than she is tall, and she holds it high above her head. The wind catches it, spreading the cloth on a glorious flare.

At that moment, the rain starts. The sun still visible between the clouds. A rainbow arcs from one side of the valley to the other. From a red underskirt to a yellow pennant. Something changes forever. She is not sure what, but something happened. The earth shifted its path a little.

The next morning, on their way to the sunrise ceremony, Aksil slips out of her hand. "Come here!" she shouts after him as he darts through the alleyways and straight towards The Wall. "Stop!" she calls in alarm as he runs headlong into it. And disappears. A moment later he runs back through the stone, a little further down The Wall. She gasps and others in the crowd start to notice.

As the grey dawn warms to a deep red sunrise, more and more of the children join in the game. They are running through The Wall as if it didn't exist.

The adults struggle with fear and confusion. What is happening? They rush to protect their offspring from the terrible danger of Those People, but the children are too delighted with their newfound freedom to stop. Laughing and shouting they dip in and out of their town and whatever horrors lie beyond the wall. And wait, some of them are not children the people know. Still in their night clothes. They look like normal children but, no, they can't be.

"Those People's children are in our town!" roars the butcher.

Chaos breaks out. Some people try to catch or chase the children from the other side of The Wall. But somehow their joy at the new game is too much. They are unstoppable.

Part 6:
Now walk through walls...Epilogue: The Wall of War

After what feels like a long time, Kahina walks towards the wall. Calmly, purposefully, confidently. "I can," she thinks. "We can." She walks straight through the stone as if it was just a cloud. And straight into the waiting arms of Izil.

"Is it you?" she asks.

"We are here," he answers. "Our rainbow melted the wall. Now we can see that you are like us and you can see that we are like you."

Part 6:
Now walk through walls...Gratitudes

Gratitudes

On my way to writing this book I have been lucky enough to have some extraordinary opportunities.

The corporate world took a chance on employing a left wing, Northern female from a low status school at a time when most candidates were none of those things. And then listened when I argued that women needed just the same opportunities, meaning I got to travel to countries I hadn't even heard of, learn a lot in a short time and work with an amazing range of people from around the world.

Alec Reed took a chance on me when I wanted to take a year's sabbatical from that world to work in development. He handed over his NGO to me allowing me a crash course in development projects and fundraising. He inspired me with his energy and broad range of interests in making the world a better place.

My local community in Telegraph Hill, London, thanks to whom I sang on stage for the first time, ran my first football tournament, learnt how to forage and got used to the idea of standing at the front of the room and sharing my ideas.

Part 6:
Now walk through walls…Gratitudes

Artmongers who invited me to be a director when I knew nothing about art in adversity. We had struggles and adventures in five countries and many heart-warming moments. I learnt a very different way of problem solving than that which I was used to in the business world.

My three children who stuck with it through all our ups and downs, always having the courage to speak their truth, coaching me on inclusion and insisting I make "bold moves" when they needed me less.

The bosses who have inspired me – Marcel, Graham, Kate, Michael and Steve by daring to be different and challenge the status quo, operating in line with their principles even when that caused them trouble. Thank you for seeing things in me that I was not yet conscious of.

And the other bosses (I won't mention you by name!) who have helped me grow by showing me behaviours I wouldn't want to replicate.

The very many friends and teachers along the way who have shared their point of view with me. Some from the other sides of walls, some from a different place on the same side. For every late night conversation that made me

Part 6:
Now walk through walls…Gratitudes

think, opened my eyes, gave me new ways to see the world.

The island of Bali who healed, inspired and nourished while I wrote this book. Including the staff at Warung Lala & Lili in Ubud, Bali who kept me safe, fed and housed.

And of course, I honour every one of those walls I have walked through! Each one had a gift for me. I scuffed my knees and banged my head but every journey through a wall was worth it for the bright light and new possibilities on the other side.

> *"Magic is believing in yourself, if you can do that, you can make anything happen."*

Goethe

Made in the USA
Columbia, SC
20 September 2022

67665624R00111